Handbook for Evaluating and Selecting Curriculum Materials

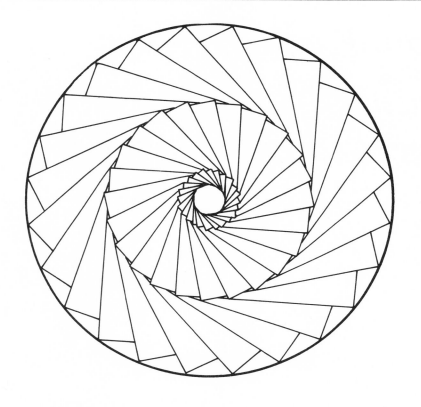

Handbook for Evaluating and Selecting Curriculum Materials

Meredith Damien Gall
University of Oregon

ALLYN AND BACON, INC.
Boston   London   Sydney   Toronto

Library of Congress Cataloging in Publication Data

Gall, Meredith D   1942–
    Handbook for evaluating and selecting curriculum materials.

        Bibliography: p.
        Includes index.
        1. Curriculum planning.   2. Teaching — Aids and devices — Evaluation.   I. Title.
LB1570.G343   375'.001   80–22114
ISBN 0–205–07294–1
ISBN 0–205–07301–8–(pbk.)

Series Editor: Margaret Quinlin

10   9   8   7   6   5   4   3   2   86   85

Printed in the United States of America

To Joyce and Jonathan

Contents

List of Tables

List of Figures

Foreword

Hucksters promote good and poor curriculum materials in equally strident voices. Some of the best, most imaginative material is somehow concealed in obscure places. Those who would choose high quality materials relevant to the objectives and processes of their curriculums have no mean task.

Meredith Gall's new book is designed to help educators find sources for curriculum materials and once the materials are located, to analyse them and select the ones most appropriate to their goals. Gall presents a typology of materials and a series of steps that can be used in proceeding from awareness of curricular needs all the way to the incorporation of the materials into the curriculum. Both the typology and the steps are carefully thought out and are eminently practical. They provide discipline in a very important area which has hitherto been marked by rule of thumb decisions made in a chaotic marketplace.

The author brings his considerable experience as an instructional materials-developer to bear on the problem area. The criteria he presents in his paradigm go beyond the analysis of content and process to the development of sensitivity to the kinds of biases that have been such familiar defects in so many materials that have been available for schools. The careful application of his criteria should result in the reduction of both sex and ethnic bias, the promotions of advertisers, and the value-biases of publishers and authors themselves.

Children spend twelve years of their lives working with instructional materials. A large proportion of instruction is built around print and audio-visual media. The recent developments in computers, video displays, and self-pacing programing may even increase the portion of media-related instructional time. Thus, selecting the best available for every curricular and instructional purpose is a matter of considerable importance. Most schools and school districts could vastly improve their procedures for involving teachers and curriculum specialists in the assembly of potential materials and the arduous process of winnowing the wheat from the chaff. This handbook is a concise presentation of the general procedures for doing this job well.

The selection of curriculum objectives has received much careful attention, and taxonomies are available to clarify objectives. The instructional process, which relies so heavily on the curriculum materials used, is in similar need of clear definition. But, before Gall's clear and concise paradigm, the field of curriculum materials selection has lacked disciplined grounding.

Bruce R. Joyce

A Note to Teachers, Curriculum Specialists, Administrators, and Professors

Knowing how to select curriculum materials is an essential skill for the professional educator. *If you are a teacher*, this handbook can help you in selecting your own materials and when serving on materials selection committees. You will find the access section of the *Handbook* especially useful in providing information on a wide range of curriculum materials available for classroom use.

As a curriculum specialist, responsible for selecting and purchasing materials, you also are likely to be called on as an expert resource to teachers in their search for curriculum materials. This handbook can be used as a reference tool to assist you in each aspect of the selection process: identifying curriculum materials, analyzing and evaluating them, and making adoption decisions.

Administrators, too, have major responsibility for curriculum materials selection. Purchase of curriculum materials is a significant item in school budgets, and school boards expect that appropriations will be spent to purchase high quality, cost-effective materials. *If you are an administrator*, the *Handbook* should assist you in making sound selection decisions. The chapters on procedures for evaluating materials and for making adoption decisions should be especially helpful.

An important goal of college and university teacher education programs is to train new and returning teachers in techniques for selecting effective curriculum materials to meet the needs of students. *If you are a professor* in a teacher education program, you can consider using the *Handbook* to achieve this goal. As students progress through the *Handbook*, they can be given assignments to identify, analyze, and evaluate materials in curriculum areas for which they have teaching responsibility.

Another use of the *Handbook* is in courses to prepare curriculum specialists, for example, as a text in a course on curriculum development or curriculum theory. Should you wish to place more stress on the process of selecting curriculum materials, there is sufficient content in the *Handbook* to cover a semester or quarter course on this topic. A useful activity is to have one or two students each class session present an analysis and evaluation of a curriculum product. This activity exposes the whole class to a wide range of curriculum content and gives them additional practice in material analysis and evaluation. References are provided at the end of each chapter to help you and your students explore particular topics in more depth.

Acknowledgments

I was unfamiliar with most of the techniques and resources in this handbook when I first started teaching the course *CI 567: Curriculum Materials* at the University of Oregon in 1975. Students who have taken the course — teachers, administrators, curriculum specialists — taught me much about curriculum materials selection based on their personal experiences and research. In a very real sense my students (with a special nod to Ann Russell and Harbans Narang) have been my collaborators in preparing this book.

I owe a special debt to Laurene Zaporozhetz, a member of the University of Oregon's Library faculty. Her expertise in curriculum librarianship was invaluable to me in correcting factual errors, in identifying resources not generally known to educators, and in formulating the role that curriculum librarians can and should play in the materials selection process. Thank you, Laurene.

Several colleagues shared freely of their ideas and experience as I was developing the manuscript. I wish especially to acknowledge Rosemarie Service, library faculty member at the University of Oregon, Bev Malugin, curriculum materials specialist with the Eugene School District, David Elliott, West Coast director of Educational Products Information Exchange, and Marda Woodbury, distinguished curriculum librarian and author. Richard Hersh, associate dean for teacher education at the University of Oregon, Christopher Clark, professor at Michigan State University, and Bruce Joyce, distinguished educator and researcher, gave me early encouragement to undertake this venture.

Virginia Williams and Sissel Lemke typed several drafts of the manuscript. Their prompt and accurate work was a great help in the production of the manuscript.

Handbook for
Evaluating and Selecting
Curriculum Materials

1   *Introduction*

Educators who want to be more effective should ensure that their students are provided with quality curriculum materials. Curriculum materials play an important role in instruction and therefore should be selected carefully. This chapter introduces an effective, systematic process for evaluating and selecting curriculum materials and explains how the rest of the handbook is organized around the basic steps of this process.

The Need for This Handbook

Selection of good curriculum materials is an important part of the total instructional process. Increasingly, educators are realizing that the content and quality of curriculum materials influence not only what students learn but how well they learn it. Educators also usually spend a great deal of effort developing a curriculum philosophy and goals for their school districts. If these efforts are not accompanied by a careful materials selection process, the district may wind up purchasing materials that subvert or otherwise fail to achieve its curriculum goals.

This emphasis on the importance of curriculum materials and a careful selection process are not intended to minimize the teacher's role. A good teacher is essential for effective instruction, but even good teachers are helped or hindered by the available curriculum materials.

Although educators generally agree that curriculum materials are important, the actual process of selecting them is often haphazard, hasty, superficial, or simply nonexistent. A major cause of this problem is that educators have not been systematically trained to select curriculum materials. Systematic training should cover the four A's of materials selection: access, analysis, appraisal, and adoption, discussed in separate chapters later on. The recognition that educators are generally unfamiliar with these four processes led to the development of this handbook. Its purpose is to provide a resource for educators, curriculum specialists, and administrators who want to improve their skill in accessing, analyzing, appraising, and adopting curriculum materials. (See Figure 1.)

In preparing the handbook, I found that while a large number of catalogs, techniques, and services have been developed to improve the curriculum materials selection process, these valuable resources are scattered through the professional literature. Until now, they have not been brought together in the form of a single, comprehensive handbook or organized into a coherent discipline. The *Handbook* is an effort to define the discipline of curriculum materials selection and to describe what is known about it.

Many curriculum materials are created by teachers for their own use; many others are published for general distribution by commercial pub-

FIGURE 1   Steps in the Process of Adopting Curriculum Materials
(See Chapter Two)

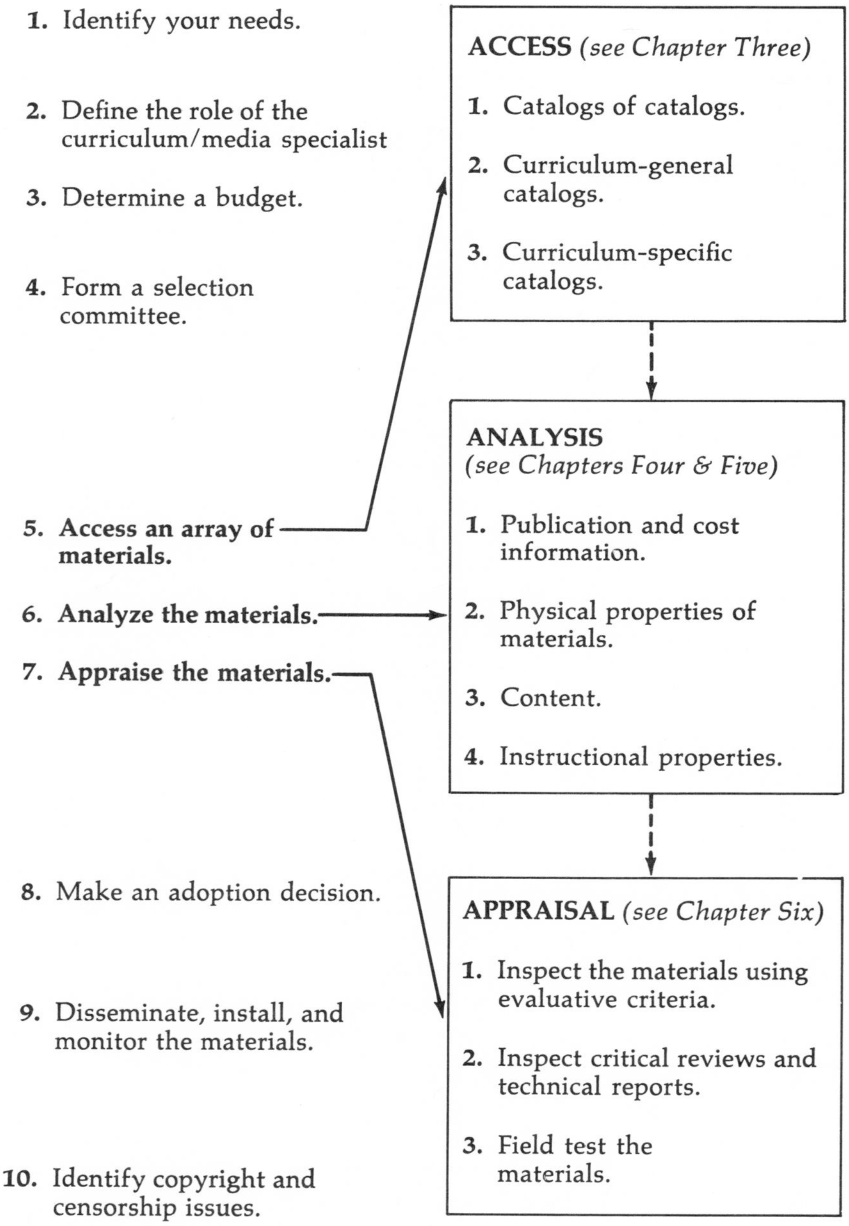

1. Identify your needs.

2. Define the role of the curriculum/media specialist

3. Determine a budget.

4. Form a selection committee.

ACCESS *(see Chapter Three)*

1. Catalogs of catalogs.

2. Curriculum-general catalogs.

3. Curriculum-specific catalogs.

5. **Access an array of materials.**

6. **Analyze the materials.**

7. **Appraise the materials.**

ANALYSIS
(see Chapters Four & Five)

1. Publication and cost information.

2. Physical properties of materials.

3. Content.

4. Instructional properties.

8. Make an adoption decision.

9. Disseminate, install, and monitor the materials.

10. Identify copyright and censorship issues.

APPRAISAL *(see Chapter Six)*

1. Inspect the materials using evaluative criteria.

2. Inspect critical reviews and technical reports.

3. Field test the materials.

lishers, nonprofit educational agencies, businesses, and other organizations. The *Handbook* is concerned with the latter, that is, published materials generally available to educators. The *Handbook* also considers all manner of curriculum materials — irrespective of content, grade level, or media format.

What Are Curriculum Materials?

Education professionals tend to think of curriculum materials as the textbooks, pamphlets, films, slides/tapes, and so on, used in instruction. A more technical definition is as follows: *Curriculum materials are physical entities, representational in nature, used to facilitate the learning process.*

The term, "physical entities," means that curriculum materials are observable objects, not ideas and concepts. Thus, instructional objectives are not curriculum materials because they are not observable objects. Textbooks and other assorted printed matter — workbooks, pamphlets, teachers' mimeographed handouts, films and filmstrips, audiotapes, and games — are the most common physical forms of curriculum materials.

Another characteristic of curriculum materials is that their intent is to facilitate learning. For example, textbooks are generally used for instructional purposes and therefore are properly classified as curriculum materials. If a textbook is used as a doorstop or paperweight, however, it ceases to be curriculum material for it no longer satisfies the definitional requirement of facilitating the learning process. Some materials, such as some historical novels, are designed primarily to entertain the reader. Under certain conditions, they also could be used for instructional purposes; if so, they would be classified as curriculum materials according to the definition presented here.

The "representational" nature of curriculum materials means that they signify something other than themselves. For example, a history textbook has no instructional significance in itself. As a physical object, it is simply a collection of printed pages held together by a binding and cover. The history textbook acquires instructional significance because the printed text is used to *represent* historical events and ideas about those events. Similarly, films and audiotapes are representational in that they provide visual or auditory representations of people, things, or ideas.

The representational nature of curriculum materials distinguishes them from *curriculum supplies*. Paper, pencils, scissors, certain types of scientific apparatus, biological organisms, and automobiles in driver education classes are examples of curriculum supplies rather than of curriculum materials because, even though they support the learning process, they do not represent anything other than themselves. The field of curriculum supplies is large and has a significant role in education. The field of curriculum materials, however, is equally large and therefore the *Handbook* is dedicated entirely to the process involved in selecting them.

Organization of the Handbook

The *Handbook* is organized according to the four A's — the four basic processes of curriculum materials selection:

Access: the search for curriculum materials to meet a particular need.

Analysis: breakdown and description of the components of a particular set of curriculum materials.

Appraisal: evaluation of the quality and effectiveness of curriculum materials.

Adoption: selection and purchase of a particular set of curriculum materials.

The four processes of curriculum materials selection ideally follow a temporal sequence. First, one would identify the available range of materials (access) to meet a particular curriculum need. Next, one would describe what these materials are like (analysis). Having described the materials thoroughly, one then has a sound basis for judging their worth (appraisal). And finally, having completed the preceding steps, one decides which of the materials to purchase (adoption).

Curriculum-General vs. Curriculum-Specific Resources

In thinking about curriculum, some educators find it useful to distinguish between that which is *general* to many content areas of the curriculum and that which is *specific* to a particular content area. For example, the technique of formulating behavioral objectives can be applied to many curriculum subjects. In contrast, the teaching of regrouping principles in addition and subtraction is a specific concern of the mathematics curriculum specialist.

The same distinction applies to the field of curriculum materials selection. Many of the catalogs, services, and techniques described in Chapter 3 are intended for a wide spectrum of curriculum content. Other access resources are limited in application to one type of curriculum content, e.g., reading, mathematics, and biology. Similarly, in Chapter 6 there are separate sections on curriculum-general evaluation checklists and curriculum-specific evaluation checklists.

The choice of a curriculum-general or curriculum-specific resource will depend upon your needs. If you intend only to evaluate fifth-grade social studies materials, it's best to select a "tailor-made" evaluation checklist designed specifically for social studies content. If you need to evaluate curriculum materials spanning a variety of content areas, however, a general evaluation checklist might be more useful.

The Relative Importance of Materials in Instruction

Some educators claim that good teachers do not need "store bought" curriculum materials. Good teachers rely on their own knowledge and enthusiasm, supplemented perhaps by a few improvised materials, to spark the learning process.

Another camp of educators believes that most teachers are not gifted, and therefore it is important to provide them with high quality curriculum materials. This view led to the development of so-called "teacher proof" curriculum materials in the 1950's and 1960's. These are materials that can be used effectively irrespective of the teacher's ability or biases.

Still another viewpoint is that neither teachers nor curriculum materials are important. If students are just left alone, they will learn by themselves. And there is no need for curriculum materials, because the real world itself is the curriculum. For example, if students wish to learn about a particular country, send them to that country so that they can experience it firsthand, rather than having them read about it in a dull textbook within the confines of a sterile classroom.

What is the proper role of curriculum materials in instruction? To what extent should teachers rely on them in the process of helping students acquire new knowledge, skills, and attitudes?

Research does not suggest a clear answer to these questions. The most we can say at this time is that the role of curriculum materials differs with each teaching situation, varying with the learning outcomes desired, the teacher, the students, and the situational context. In designing any form of instruction, we can view the teacher and curriculum materials as two *resources* that can be drawn upon to help students learn. The teacher alone will be sufficient for some instructional tasks; for others, curriculum materials will be sufficient. Or perhaps a mix of the two will be desirable.

Figure 1 illustrates the interplay of teacher and curriculum materials as two types of instructional resources. In class discussions (see Figure 2a)

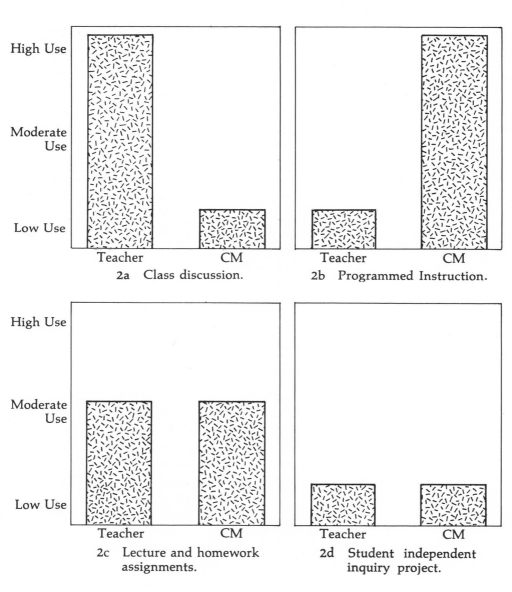

FIGURE 2   Examples of How Teachers and Curriculum Materials Vary as Instructional Resources

2a   Class discussion.

2b   Programmed Instruction.

2c   Lecture and homework assignments.

2d   Student independent inquiry project.

the teacher is the primary resource. He or she moderates the verbal interaction and introduces information when appropriate. Curriculum materials typically play relatively little or no role in this method of instruction. In contrast, curriculum materials play a prominent role in programmed instruction (see Figure 2b), where the teacher's role is secondary.

One of the most common methods of instruction, especially in secondary education, is teacher lecture accompanied by homework assignments. Both teacher and curriculum materials play important, complementary roles in this method (see Figure 2c).

The last example is the method of independent inquiry (Figure 2d). Students may be asked to formulate a research problem and to collect relevant data. Depending upon the student's level of independence, the teacher may provide relatively little assistance while the research is in progress. In some projects, the primary requirement is for the student to collect original data and present them in a report. Under these conditions, the roles of the teacher and curriculum materials, while necessary to the instructional process, are subservient to the student's own inquiry process. Thus, the extent of the contribution of curriculum materials varies with the instructional task.

Selection of Curriculum Materials as a Strategy for School Improvement

Among the many strategies for improving schools is the introduction of new curriculum materials into the school program. If this strategy is chosen, there must be a specific method for implementing it. One major method is for school districts to *develop* their own materials. This is often done by paying teachers, during the summer break, to create materials in accordance with district curriculum goals. Another method is for school districts to *select* from among published curriculum materials.

It is beyond the scope of the *Handbook* to consider the relative merits of these methods. I wish only to emphasize that curriculum materials selection is *one* viable method of bringing about school improvement and change.

If materials selection becomes a focus for school improvement, in-service education also should be focused in this direction. For example, teacher training in selection procedures is especially important because teachers are not likely to learn systematic procedures for selecting materials in preservice programs (1). Teachers should also become reacquainted with the district's curriculum philosophy and goals so that materials are selected in accordance with them.

A related focus for in-service education is providing teachers the opportunity to review new curriculum materials for possible adoption. A recent survey of in-service teachers found that examination of new materials ranked highest in preference among the services that a Teacher Center might provide (2).

Research About Curriculum Materials and Their Selection

Until quite recently, researchers devoted little effort to the study of curriculum materials and the process by which they are selected. Instead, most efforts were directed toward the study of teachers — teacher education, teacher characteristics, classroom interaction with students, and teaching methods.

The priority given to research on teachers, rather than to research on curriculum materials, is quite understandable. The teacher is, after all, the most prominent feature of classroom instruction: teachers are human, dynamic, and intriguing; materials are lifeless and sometimes dull. In addition, salaries and related expenses for teachers constitute well over half of the typical school budget, whereas purchase of materials seldom exceeds one or two percent of total expenditures (3). Finally, teachers are part of the public sector and thus are generally accessible for investigation by researchers. In contrast, the development and distribution of curriculum materials have been controlled largely by private publishing firms, which are not as open to research study.

Although the research base is small, we can glean from it a few tentative generalizations about the role of curriculum materials in instruction:

1. *Instruction is largely determined by the content of curriculum materials.* With respect to mathematics education, Stake and Easley (4) found that the main source of knowledge in instruction is the textbook. Teachers generally rely on a single textbook and its supplemental teacher's manual, suggesting that teachers generally do not introduce content of their own choosing into classroom instruction. Thus, materials determine the school curriculum, probably more so than district-level or school-level objectives.

2. *Students spend much of their time interacting with curriculum materials rather than with the teacher.* Recent research indicates that elementary school students spend a large part of their time in classrooms doing "seatwork" rather than engaged in verbal interaction with teachers (5). A national survey of 13,000 K–12 teachers found that they use instructional materials, print and nonprint, during 90 to 95 percent of their instructional time (6). Seatwork generally involves

silent reading assignments or workbook activity. As students progress through school, the percentage of time that students interact with materials probably increases. For example, homework assignments — which typically involve study of curriculum materials — generally become longer. At the college level it is not uncommon for students to spend three or four hours in outside study for every hour in class.

3. *Materials that appear to have the same purpose may differ substantially in content coverage.* A recent analysis of fourth grade mathematics textbooks (7) indicated that they differed from each other in important ways. Many topics found in one textbook were not found in the other textbooks; many of the "core" topics common to all of the textbooks varied in the amount of emphasis that they were given. These findings, although limited to one aspect of the K–12 curriculum, suggest the importance of carefully examining the content of materials before making an adoption decision.

Another set of research findings is relevant to the process of curriculum materials selection. These findings are as follows:

1. *Curriculum materials are not likely to be evaluated and revised prior to publication.* Studies by the Educational Product Information Exchange (EPIE) revealed that less than one percent of the half million or so curriculum materials sold by the publishing industry have ever been field-tested with children and revised prior to publication (8). Some curriculum areas are worse in this respect than others. For example, only three of the 223 materials most often used in broadcast video instruction were field-tested prior to publication. This lack of field-testing implies that many curriculum materials on the market are of unknown effectiveness. Thus, educators have a heavy responsibility to screen materials carefully before making selection decisions.

2. *Teachers limit their search for curriculum materials to those that are immediately available.* A recent study by Christopher Clark and his associates (9) found that teachers tend to limit their search for ideas to immediately available materials, for example, the teacher edition of textbooks, magazine articles, and films. This research finding suggests that a careful survey of available materials, using the *access* procedures described in Chapter 3, serves to expand the teacher's range of options for classroom instruction.

3. *Teachers spend relatively little of their time engaged in the process of materials selection.* The recent survey by the EPIE Institute (10) found that nearly half (45 percent) of the sampled teachers have no role in choosing the instructional materials they are required to use. Of those

teachers involved in materials selection, the majority of them (54 percent) report that they spend less than one hour per year in this process. Teachers' lack of involvement in selecting materials seems inconsistent with the actual importance of materials in instruction.

4. *Teachers are not well informed about the process of curriculum materials selection.* Another finding of the same EPIE survey is that the average teacher has not been trained to evaluate or to select materials for classroom use. This lack of preparation helps to explain why teachers usually limit their choices to readily available materials and why they spend little time in the selection process. These findings dramatize the need for teacher in-service and pre-service training in the major processes of curriculum materials selection: access, analysis, appraisal, and adoption.

The Relationship Between Curriculum Development and Curriculum Materials Selection

James Popham and Eva Baker define curriculum as "all the planned learning outcomes for which the school is responsible" (11). This definition highlights the major purpose of curriculum development: to identify the broad goals and more specific objectives that instruction should strive to achieve. For example, a common, broad, curriculum goal is to help students become law-abiding, active citizens in society.

The formulation of curriculum goals and objectives is usually based on some conception of the nature of learning, the learner, and society. John McNeil has identified four contrasting conceptions that guide much of contemporary curriculum development (12): humanism, social reconstructionism, instructional technology, and academic discipline orientation. For example, curriculum developers with a humanistic viewpoint tend to formulate instructional goals that reflect a belief in the individual's need for *personal* growth and integrity. In contrast, social reconstructionists stress instructional goals that give students the capability to effect *social* reform.

Another major purpose of curriculum development is to sequence instructional objectives so that students develop an interconnected progression of skills and knowledge through their school years. This aspect of curriculum development usually results in scope and sequence charts, spiral structures, developmentally-based sequences, or other curriculum organizations.

Once curriculum objectives and sequences are specified, the next logical step is to specify means for implementing them. At this point the selection of appropriate curriculum materials should become a major concern. Some curriculum developers stop at this point, for their curriculum guides contain goals, objectives, and sequences but no list of materials and teaching methods for implementing them. When this situation occurs, it is easy for curriculum materials selection to become detached from the total curriculum development process. As a result, some materials adoption committees and individual teachers are unable to justify their selections in terms of a larger conception of curriculum, as specified perhaps by the school district or state department of education.

Lack of coordination between curriculum objectives and materials selection can be avoided if curriculum development is viewed as a total, integrated process that includes material selection as one of its steps. One way to insure this integrated process is to have one group of educators formulate all aspects of curriculum development, including goals and objectives, sequencing, materials, teaching methods, and evaluation. This approach is rarely practiced except for small parts of the curriculum, however, because of the large amounts of time required of individual educators. Instead, school districts usually form several or many committees and departments, each responsible for a different aspect of curriculum development.

If different committees and departments are to yield an integrated curriculum, it is important that each group be aware of the others' efforts. Thus, materials selection committees and individual teachers should carefully review relevant curriculum guides developed by the school district before they access, analyze, or evaluate any materials. If materials are selected in disregard of the larger curriculum, the result is likely to be a disconnected instructional program that fractionates students' learning opportunities rather than allowing them to build one upon the other.

CHAPTER 1 Notes

1. Robert E. Stake and Jack A. Easley, *Case Studies in Science Education* (Washington, D.C.: National Science Foundation, 1978); "National Survey and Assessment of Instructional Materials: Two Years Later," *EPIEgram* 5 (1976): 1–3.

2. Roy C. Rodriguez, Dianne S. Mancus, and J. Richard Suchman, "A Teacher Center Consortium for Rural School Districts: Goals and Rationale," *NSPI Journal* 12 (1978):23–25.

3. The national survey conducted by Educational Products Information Exchange found that less than one percent (.97) of the average school district's budget is spent on instructional materials. Reported in *EPIEgram* 6 (1978):4.

4. Stake and Easley, op. cit.

5. Barak V. Rosenshine, "Content, Time, and Direction Instruction," in *Research on Teaching: Concepts, Findings, and Implications*, ed. Penelope L. Peterson and Herbert J. Walbert (Berkeley, Calif.: McCutchan, 1979):28–56.

6. National survey and assessment, *op. cit.*

7. Therese M. Kuhs and Donald J. Freeman, *The Potential Influence of Textbooks on Teachers' Selection of Content for Elementary School Mathematics* (East Lansing: Michigan State University, Institute for Research for Teaching, 1979) Research Series No. 48.

8. "How to Tell Whether Your Schools Are Being Gypped, *The American School Board Journal* 162 (1975):38–40.

9. The Institute for Research on Teaching, Michigan State University, *Communication Quarterly* 1, no. 4 (1978):1.

10. National survey and assessment, *op. cit.*

11. W. James Popham and Eva L. Baker, *Systematic Instruction* (Englewood Cliffs, N.J.: Prentice-Hall, 1970):48.

12. John D. McNeill, *Curriculum: A Comprehensive Introduction* (Boston: Little, Brown, 1977).

CHAPTER 1   Bibliography

Anderson, Robert M.; Greer, John G.; and Odle, Sara J., ed. *Individualizing Educational Materials for Special Children in the Mainstream*. Baltimore, Md.: University Park Press, 1978.

Association for Educational Communications and Technology. *Selecting Media for Learning: Readings from Audiovisual Instruction*. Washington, D.C.: AECT, 1974.

Educational Products Information Exchange. *Report on a National Study of the Nature and the Quality of Instructional Materials Most Used by Teachers and Learners*. Report No. 76. New York: EPIE, 1976.

Joint Committee of the National Education Association and Association of American Publishers. *Selecting Instructional Materials for Purchase*. Washington, D.C.: National Education Association, 1972.

Klein, M. Frances. *About Learning Materials*. Washington, D.C.: Association for Supervision and Curriculum Development, 1978.

Kunder, Linda H. *Procedures for Textbook and Instructional Materials Selection*. Arlington Va.: Educational Research Service, 1976.

Talmage, Harriet. "The Textbook as Arbiter of Curriculum and Instruction." *The Elementary School Journal* 73 (1972):20–25.

Woodbury, Marda. *Selecting Instructional Materials.* Fastback 110. Bloomington, Ind.: Phi Delta Kappa, 1978.

———. *Selecting Materials for Instruction: Issues and Policies.* Littleton, Colo.: Libraries Unlimited, 1979.

———. *Selecting Materials for Instruction: Media and the Curriculum.* Littleton, Colo.: Libraries Unlimited, in press.

———. *Selecting Materials for Instruction: Subject Areas and Implementation.* Littleton, Colo.: Libraries Unlimited, in press.

2 Steps in Adopting Curriculum Materials

Have you ever been appointed to a textbook or media selection committee? Have you wondered how to make good selections from the materials available? This chapter presents a sequence of nine key steps in selecting curriculum materials, three of which (5, 6, and 7) are described more fully in subsequent chapters. This chapter ends with a discussion of copyright and censorship issues that sometimes arise in selecting and using materials.

Types of Curriculum Materials Adoption

The process of curriculum materials adoption culminates in a *decision* to select, or to recommend the selection of, a particular set of materials. The adoption process can vary with respect to (1) who is making the adoption decision, (2) who is to be the recipient of the decision, and (3) the nature of the decision itself.

You can select materials either for yourself as the recipient or for other teachers to use. If you are selecting materials for your own use, the selection process should be systematic and responsible; however, it need not be very formal, with each step documented and cross-checked by others. An informal process is justified because you are accountable only to yourself, your students, and the school's curriculum policy. Try to spend some time on each of the steps outlined in the next section of this chapter, especially the steps concerning identification of needs, access, analysis, appraisal, and monitoring.

If you are selecting materials for other teachers, you probably will do so as a member of a selection committee. The committee's scope may be limited to selecting materials for use by the school district's teachers. If you are on a state committee, however, your decisions will affect teachers all over the state. In these situations, you are accountable to other teachers and their students; thus, you need to demonstrate that you have engaged in a responsible selection process. The more teachers affected by the adoption decision, the more formal the process will be.

The nature of the adoption decision also has an effect on the selection process used. There are at least three types of adoption decisions:

1. The decision may involve selecting one curriculum product from an array of products. This type of decision is usually made by a selection committee.

2. The decision may involve selecting one curriculum product, considering it on its own merits without comparing it to other products. This type of decision may be made by a teacher who comes across a new product and wishes to consider it for supplementary instruction.

3. The decision may involve forming an approved list of curriculum materials. *All* materials that satisfy certain criteria are eligible for the list. The formation of an approved list implies that more than one product can be selected by the adoption committee.

Figure 3 shows the method used by each state to select curriculum materials for public school use (1). The majority of the states (a total of 27) allow local school districts to make their own selections. Another substantial group of states (17 in all) adopts materials at the state level, with very limited flexibility given to local districts. Four states allow local district choice from an approved list having multiple options. Two states, California and West Virginia, have a dual selection procedure whereby elementary school materials are chosen from a state-approved list, and high school materials are chosen by local school districts.

Although various types of decisions can be made, the selection process for all is fairly similar. The next section presents a generic set of steps that you can adapt to meet your own needs.

The Basic Process of Selecting Materials

The following sequence for selecting curriculum materials represents an ideal model. In actual practice, some steps may be carried out concurrently or omitted. Even when time is short, I recommend that you give some thought to each step, to avoid making a hasty decision that will be later regretted.

Step 1. Identify Your Needs

Evaluation experts define a "need" as a discrepancy between an actual state and a desired state. With respect to materials, the actual state may be as obvious as a total lack of curriculum materials to meet a school district's instructional objectives. The desired state is equally obvious: the selection of materials that will enable students to achieve the instructional objectives.

The need for new materials sometimes is less dramatic. A teacher already may have materials to meet a need, but over time he or she becomes dissatisfied with them. The materials may have become dated or lack sufficient practice exercises. The search for new materials may arise from a need to correct deficiencies in current materials or just out of curiosity to see what's new on the market.

The fact that materials wear out is used by many school districts as an opportunity to rethink curriculum needs. For example, new textbooks

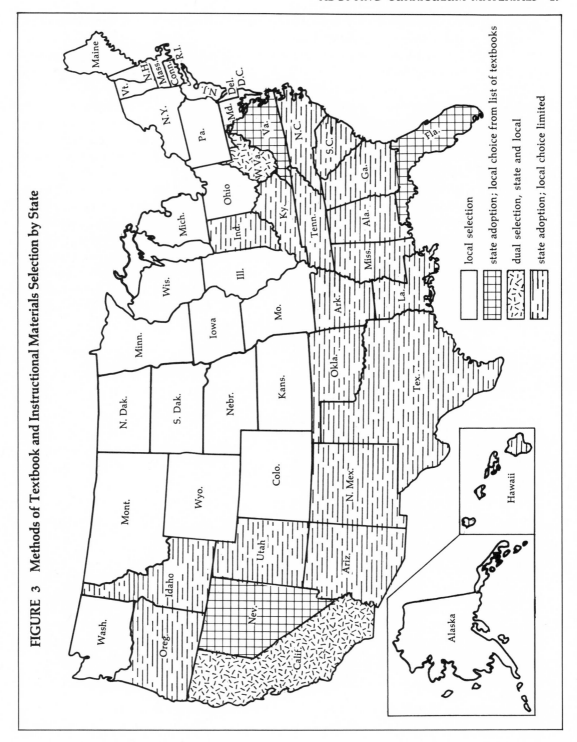

FIGURE 3 Methods of Textbook and Instructional Materials Selection by State

are usually selected every five to seven years, because this is the average durability of hardbound books in daily use.

A teacher or selection committee might consider conducting a simple, informal needs assessment. The first step is to list deficiencies in the materials in current use. (Of course, this step can be omitted if you are not selecting new materials to replace those in current use.) If many teachers are using the materials to be replaced, you can obtain opinions by surveying them, using either a questionnaire or interview as the data collection tool.

The second step in the needs assessment process is the formulation of desired characteristics to provide the criteria by which you will search for, evaluate, and select a new set of materials. Some characteristics will be an obvious reaction to the dissatisfactions with the current materials. Additional desired characteristics might result from studying the school district's curriculum philosophy and curriculum goals. And finally, desired characteristics should reflect the context in which the new materials are to be used, for example, grade level of students, reading level, scope and sequence of the curriculum, cost constraints. The analytic framework in Chapter 4 or the list of evaluative criteria in Chapter 6 will help you to specify desired characteristics of materials.

Step 2. Define the Role of the Curriculum/Media Specialist

If the selection process is to occur within a school district or State Department of Education, you probably will have access to the services of a curriculum or media specialist. The specialist may be expert in particular curriculum content areas, grade levels, or the process of materials selection. It is doubtful whether specialists should ever take sole responsibility for selecting materials, because they are too removed from the regular classroom teaching process (even though they once may have taught), and their selections may lack credibility with practicing teachers. However, a well-trained specialist can perform several important roles in the materials selection process, including these:

1.   Collect needs assessment data relating to teacher dissatisfaction with current materials and characteristics desired of new materials.

2.   Access an array of materials for the teacher or committee to examine.

3.   Pre-analyze the materials.

4.   Assist the teacher or committee in formulating evaluative criteria.

5.   Answer teachers' technical questions about the materials.

6. Facilitate and participate in committee meetings and in the decision-making process. This role is critical to the success of the adoption process.

Curriculum or media specialists may be called upon to perform one, some, or all of these functions. They also may have responsibility for delegating these roles to other persons involved in the selection process.

Step 3. Determine a Budget

An informal selection process conducted by one or two teachers does not usually require a detailed budget. The array of materials from which a selection will be made is generally small, and the cost of postage and copies of materials is negligible.

As the selection process increases in scope and complexity, the costs also increase to the point that a budget should be planned. For example, a state textbook adoption committee might spend thousands of dollars to complete its assigned tasks. Budget items include teacher time (extra duty pay or payment of substitute teachers); travel reimbursement for committee members to attend meetings; postage and other communication costs; copies of materials not provided free or on approval by publishers; duplication of analysis and evaluation forms; materials catalogs and reference works; and curriculum consultants.

If you have responsibility for budget preparation in your school or district, you might consider entering "materials selection" as a separate item. This procedure helps to insure that you will have the funds to engage in a responsible, thorough selection process. Even if funds cannot be set aside for every set of materials to be adopted, it should be possible to obtain sufficient funds to cover the selection of materials in high priority areas of the curriculum.

If a committee is to be used in the selection process (see step 4), costs can be reduced by including fewer members on the committee. Each additional member incurs more personnel expense, more communication costs, and so forth.

Step 4. Form a Selection Committee

The formation of a selection committee should be considered whenever the materials are to be adopted for use by more than a few teachers. If one person does the selection, teachers may feel that the process is arbitrary and biased, no matter how sound the person's judgment. A major purpose of a selection committee, then, is to reassure teachers that their perspective was represented in the adoption process.

Who should be assigned to the committee? Certainly it should include several teachers who eventually will use the adopted materials. Teacher representatives should be selected by the teachers themselves, preferably through a recognized teacher group (a local teachers union, association of social studies teachers, etc.).

The committee also should include a curriculum or media specialist. As stated in step 2, this person provides special expertise and resources to the committee.

Parents and other persons in the community should be invited to represent community perspective. Their participation is especially important of you are selecting materials to implement major elements of the school curriculum or if the materials are possibly controversial (see the section on censorship at the end of this chapter). Students, too, should be considered for inclusion on the committee; as the ultimate "consumer" of the materials, their views are important and frequently insightful. Administrators also have a valid perspective that should be represented.

A major issue is how many persons should be included on the committee. Research on group process suggests that five or six members is the optimum group size (2). A larger group than this makes it difficult for individuals to have their views heard, and, as pointed out in step 3, adoption costs increase as committee size increases. It is therefore advisable to oppose efforts to load up a committee with every conceivable person who might have an interest in the selection process. Group size can be held down by including just one, or no more than two, persons to represent each constituency affected by the adoption process.

In my experience, committees operate best if there is division of labor. One committee member should be designated the chairperson or moderator. This person has the responsibility of keeping the committee on task and working to make an adoption decision. Another person — perhaps a curriculum or media specialist — can perform much of the important work that precedes the actual selection decision. He or she can find out what materials are available to choose from, prepare analytic descriptions of materials, develop and distribute evaluation forms, and so forth. This person should be chosen on the basis of his or her expertise and willingness to make the necessary time commitment.

Because the committee members are likely to be busy people, their time should be used efficiently. The committee's input is most critical at step 1 (identification of needs), step 7 (appraisal), and step 8 (selection decision). Therefore, meetings where everyone is assembled should emphasize these steps. The other steps can be completed, to a large extent, by a person working independently or in occasional consultation with selected committee members.

Step 5. Access an Array of Materials

Selection committees, in most instances, will want to select a curriculum package from a set of alternatives. In order for the committee to engage in "comparison shopping," someone needs to assemble an array of materials which the committee member can compare. Procedures for accessing materials in a particular curriculum area are described in Chapter 3.

Step 6. Analyze the Materials

The purpose of analysis is to describe objectively the salient features of each set of materials under consideration, a step sometimes omitted by selection committees in their eagerness to judge the materials. The evaluation process will be misled if it is not based on accurate data, however. For example, one cannot judge whether a set of materials is too expensive unless one knows the precise components that make up the materials and their exact price. Procedures for analyzing curriculum materials are described in Chapters 4 and 5.

Step 7. Appraise the Materials

After an array of materials has been accessed and analyzed, it must be judged by evaluative criteria. This is the most important step of the selection process, for it is here that the selectors' critical judgment is most engaged. The process of appraisal may involve inspecting the materials themselves, reading evaluation studies of their effectiveness, or using them locally under field test conditions. Procedures for using each of these appraisal processes and a comprehensive set of evaluative criteria are described in Chapter 6.

Step 8. Make an Adoption Decision

This is the culminating step in the materials selection process. The purpose of the seven preceding steps is to prepare you for making a sound adoption decision.

The decision-making process is fairly straightforward when the teacher is selecting materials for his or her own use. The process becomes more complicated when a committee whose members represent different interest groups must make a decision that will affect many teachers. The question, What procedures can committee members use to reach an agreement on a particular set of curriculum materials? should be addressed by the committee early in the selection process.

One procedure that can be used is to have each committee member rank the different materials. The highest rated materials would receive a rank of 1, the next highest rated materials would receive a rank of 2, and so forth. The materials that receive the highest mean rank would be adopted by the committee. If the committee is free to recommend several sets of materials, they could be recommended in the order that they were ranked.

Some committees might prefer a consensus approach instead of ranking. In this approach, the committee members gradually resolve their differences of opinion by a process of discussion until they reach consensus; their goal is to reach a decision with which everyone is reasonably comfortable. The consensus approach is facilitated if each committee member states perceived strengths and weaknesses of each set of materials and the weight that they assign to each evaluative criterion. These types of statements lead to a more fruitful discussion than if committee members simply state their general likes and dislikes of materials. For example, a committee member might reject a set of materials that the other members wish to adopt because of a few weaknesses that he or she perceives in it. The other members might acknowledge these weaknesses, but may also emphasize some important strengths of the materials. The reluctant member now might agree with the committee's consensus, knowing that at least his or her views have been heard and acknowledged. In this way individuals can better appreciate the basis on which other committee members are acting in weighing strengths against weaknesses.

The purpose of consensus decision-making is to arrive at a decision which each member feels is the best decision that the *committee*, not the individual, is capable of making. For consensus decision-making to work effectively, members must be willing to subordinate personal values and beliefs, to a certain extent, to the values and beliefs of the committee as a whole.

Committees occasionally fail to make an adoption decision because they lack sufficient data. In this situation, it may be necessary to analyze the materials again (step 6). Another possibility is to repeat step 7, appraising materials. A small scale field test is an appraisal technique that often helps a committee to make the right decision.

The decision-making process is likely to drag on if the committee does not work within a time limit, which can be extended if more time is needed. The committee chairperson should take the responsibility of establishing a time frame for each step of the committee's work, including the decision-making phase. The greater the impact of the decision on teachers and students, the more time should be allocated. Also, more time may be needed when a consensus approach is used instead of a simple ranking procedure.

Step 9. Disseminate, Install, and Monitor the Materials

Since this handbook is about *selection* of materials, its major concern is with procedures relating to access, analysis, appraisal, and adoption. The question of what should happen after materials have been selected is not our concern here. A few considerations deserve mention however.

It seems obvious that news of an adoption decision should be disseminated quickly to all teachers potentially affected by it. The news bulletin should include details about the selection process, the reasons why a particular set of materials was adopted, and the impact of the adoption decision on the teacher (e.g., mandatory or optional use by the teacher). If many materials are being selected on a continuing basis, as in a school district library or materials center, a catalog — with updates — should be distributed.

Much is involved in getting the materials from the publisher or distributor into the hands of the teacher. Certainly the most important aspect of this process is provision of inservice training to help the teacher understand the materials' purpose and use. If this process is not handled effectively, the materials are likely to gather dust on teachers' shelves.

Another important step in the post-selection process is monitoring the use of the materials. A curriculum or evaluation specialist might check with teachers periodically to determine whether the materials meet expectations. Data on strengths and weaknesses of the materials can be collected to determine whether to continue distributing them. It can be very helpful to share this type of information with other teachers who are considering adoption of the materials.

Copyright Issues

The issue of copyright, the exclusive legal right to reproduce, publish, and sell the matter and form of a literary, musical, or artistic work, is fairly complex, with rules on what constitutes illegal use, fair use, or being in the public domain. Teachers who wish to photocopy materials should familiarize themselves with the prohibitions of the copyright laws to avoid infringing on them.

The U.S. Constitution grants to Congress the power to "promote the Progress of Science and useful Arts, by securing for limited Times to Authors and Inventors the exclusive Right to their respective Writings and Discoveries..." The copyright laws passed by Congress are intended to give various groups — including writers and publishers of educational materials — an *economic incentive* for engaging in their work. The Congress and courts of law do not wish to restrict unduly the dissemination and use of copyrighted materials however. The principle of *fair use* has been developed to handle this situation. Fair use means that under certain circumstances, copyrighted materials can be duplicated and used by persons who do not hold the copyright.

In 1976 Congress passed a new set of copyright laws, known officially as Public Law 94-553. (This law replaced the Copyright Law of 1909.) Section 107 of the new law limits the copyright holder's exclusive rights to his or her original work; it also defines what constitutes "fair use," as follows:

> The fair use of a copyrighted work, including such use by reproduction in copies or phonorecords or by any other means specified by that section, for purposes such as criticism, comment, news reporting, teaching (including multiple copies for classroom use), scholarship, or research, is not an infringement of copyright. In determining whether the use made of a work in any particular case is a fair use the factors to be considered shall include —
>
> 1. the purpose and character of the use, including whether such use is of a commercial nature or is for nonprofit educational purposes;
> 2. the nature of the copyrighted work;
> 3. the amount and substantiality of the portion used in relation to the copyrighted work as a whole; and
> 4. the effect of the use upon the potential market for or value of the copyrighted work.

The guidelines for fair use of copyrighted material listed under Section 107 are quite abroad. More specific guidelines were prepared by several groups concerned about copyright legalities. These guidelines, which are generally regarded as reasonable interpretations of Section 107, are presented in Appendix A. You will note that they include conditions under which teachers can make single copies of copyrighted materials for their own use or multiple copies for classroom use. These conditions require you to consider the amount of copyrighted materials to be duplicated (test of brevity); the timing of the decision to use the material (test of spontaneity);

and whether you have copied these materials or related materials previously during the class term (test of cumulative effect).

The purpose of Section 107 and its guidelines is to allow copying in situations necessary for the smooth transmission of recorded knowledge, while also protecting the economic interests of persons who have labored to develop and publish this knowledge.

The preceding discussion covers only a few aspects of the new copyright laws. Other sections of the new laws concern such procedures as copying by libraries, performance of literary and dramatic works, retransmission of material originally transmitted by a broadcast station, and reproduction of sound recordings and computer information systems. You are advised to seek counsel if you are unsure about what constitutes "fair use" of copyrighted material in a specific instructional situation. The new copyright laws are complex, and many of them require expert interpretation to determine whether one is acting in compliance with them. Also, the laws are being reviewed in 1981, and this process may lead to new provisions about what constitutes permissible copying of materials.

If your intended use of copyrighted material does not fall within "fair use" guidelines, you should seek permission from the publisher to reproduce the material. In all cases permission to use materials should be sought as soon as possible, for permission releases from publishers generally require at least a one-to-two month wait.

Permission should be requested in writing rather than by phone. In requesting permission from the publisher, you should include the following information:

1. Exact title of the material to be copied.
2. A description of what parts of the material are to be copied, e.g., specific page numbers, graphs, pictures.
3. Method of reproduction, e.g., xerox, offset.
4. Number of copies to be made.
5. Intended use of the copies.
6. Procedure for distributing the copies.
7. Price, if any, charged to students or other users.

The new copyright law states that courts cannot assess damages or other financial penalties against the innocently infringing teacher, school librarian, or other instructional specialist. In the case of the educator who knowingly infringes copyright, however, the following provisions of the new law apply:

. . . copyright infringement can result in an injunction against further violations, impoundment of wrongfully duplicated materials, actual damages suffered or 'statutory' civil damages of not less than $250 and no more than $10,000 per violation, and assessment of attorneys' fees. If the violation is extraordinary, the statutory damages can be increased to $50,000. For willful violations undertaken for financial gain, criminal penalties also can be levied. First offenders may be imprisoned for up to one year and fined up to $25,000 in addition to all the civil penalties just enumerated. (3)

Censorship Issues

The possibility of censorship should be kept in mind whenever you select curriculum materials. Censorship usually occurs after materials have been selected and purchased; members of the community, or perhaps the school board, may seek to remove them from the classroom or library. Censorship also may occur during the selection process if members of the adoption committee attempt to exclude certain materials from consideration because they find them objectionable.

A recent survey found that censorship of curriculum materials is increasing (4). In one of the surveys one-fourth of the 414 school districts in the sample had had a recent challenge to some of the materials used in their schools. The challenges occasionally are quite serious. In the highly publicized case of Kanawha County in West Virginia, community protests against curriculum materials in the schools went to the extremes of gunfire, vandalism, and burning of school property (5).

Attempts at censorship are most likely to be directed at materials that contain references to sex, use "dirty" language, or present content in conflict with certain religious beliefs (e.g., the scientific view of evolution) or American cultural values.

In a survey conducted in 1977 by the National Council of Teachers of English (6), secondary teachers reported that censorship was most often attempted against books claimed to contain obscene, vulgar language. The next most common reasons for censorship were objections to sexual references and to religious ideas presented in the books. In the same survey teachers reported that the most common reasons for objection to audiovisual materials were their references to sex, use of improper language, advocacy of certain ideas (e.g., secular humanism), or presence of violent acts.

A recent study (7) identified a list of 91 items other than textbooks that have been censored twice or more in American schools, colleges, and public libraries in the period 1966–1975. The 25 most censored items on the list are:

1. *Catcher in the Rye*
2. *Soul on Ice*
3. *Manchild in the Promised Land*
4. *Go Ask Alice*
5. *Catch-22*
6. *Nudes* (Photos and Art Works)
7. *Grapes of Wrath*
8. *Of Mice and Men*
9. *Slaughterhouse Five*
10. *To Kill a Mockingbird*
11. *Down These Mean Streets*
12. *The Godfather*
13. *Inner City Mother Goose*
14. *The Learning Tree*
15. *Lord of the Flies*
16. *Nigger*
17. *Sylvester and the Magic Pebble*
18. *Black Like Me*
19. *Deliverance*
20. *Flowers for Algernon*
21. *Lottery* (Film)
22. *Newsweek* (Magazine)
23. *One Flew Over the Cuckoo's Nest*
24. *Playboy* (Magazine)
25. *Scholastic Scope* (Magazine)

Many of these items are the objects of censorship attempts because they deal explicitly with controversial themes and use graphic language.

Persons who attempt to censor materials for the reasons cited above are sometimes labeled "conservatives" or "traditionalists." In recent years, though, we have seen an increasing occurrence of so-called "liberal" censorship. For example, "liberal" censors may seek to remove instructional materials that are sexist or racist. Critics have observed that any attempt to remove materials — even for an indisputably good cause — is censorship, and as such, is objectionable.

Many legal issues are involved in censorship of curriculum materials. For example, does the school board, or the general public, have the right to censor what a teacher may say or use as materials in the classroom? Court cases involving this issue have attempted to set guidelines that respect, on the one hand, the values of the community that supports the local schools; and on the other hand, the teacher's legitimate right to academic freedom (8). Some major organizations of educators have supported the teacher's right to freely present controversial issues and materials if the materials achieve a worthwhile educational objective that is appropriate for the students in the class (9).

Censorship problems can be avoided if the school district carefully delineates procedures and criteria for selecting its curriculum materials. Three procedures are especially important. First, the school district should include parents of students and other members of the community on the selection committee. (See step 4 of the adoption process.) In this way it will be difficult for anyone to argue that the district's educators are out of touch with community values and needs. Second, if the district plans to adopt materials that may be controversial (e.g., materials relating to sex education), the administrators should plan a campaign to educate the community about its intentions. If the adoption process is kept open and informative, hostility and challenges probably can be diffused before they erupt into a major confrontation.

The third procedure for solving censorship problems is to establish a policy for handling challenges to the district's curriculum materials. This policy should be established *before* a challenge arises. A recent survey (10) found that approximately one-third of responding school districts do not have such a policy.

A customary procedure among districts with established policies is to develop a standard form on which complaints can be registered. The very process of completing the form may cause the person to reconsider whether he or she wishes to file a complaint. If the form is completed, district administrators can respond to the person's specific criticisms rather than to global, emotional charges that the material is "socialistic," "obscene," "irreligious," etc. An example of a school district policy and form for handling complaints about curriculum materials is shown in Appendix B. You also may wish to refer to the publication *Censorship: The Challenge to Freedom in the School* sponsored by the American Association of School Administrators, Association for Supervision and Curriculum Development, National Association of Elementary School Principals, and National Association of Secondary School Principals (11). This publication provides sample policy statements, procedures, and forms that can be used by school districts to avoid or deal with censorship attempts.

CHAPTER 2 Notes

1. Linda H. Kunder, *Procedures for Textbook and Instructional Materials Selection* (Arlington, Va.: Educational Research Service, 1976):5.

2. Meredith D. Gall and Joyce P. Gall, "The Discussion Method," in *The Psychology of Teaching Methods: The Seventy-fifth Yearbook of the National Society for the Study of Education* ed. N. L. Gage (Chicago: University of Chicago Press, 1976).

3. Joint Project of American Library Association, National Council of Teachers of English, and National Education Association. *The New Copyright Law: Questions Teachers and Librarians Ask* (Chicago: American Library Association, 1977):67.

4. Kunder, *op. cit.*

5. George Hillocks, Jr. "Books and Bombs: Ideological Conflict and the Schools: A Case Study of the Kanawha County Book Protest," *School Review 86* (1978):632–654.

6. Lee Burress, "A Brief Report of the 1977 NCTE Censorship Survey," in *Dealing with Censorship,* ed. James E. Davis (Urbana, Ill.: National Council of Teachers of English, 1979):14–47.

7. L. B. Woods, "The Most Censored Materials in the U.S.," *Library Journal* 103 (1978):2170–2173. See also: L. B. Woods, "Patterns in the Censorship of Children's Materials," *Newsletter on Intellectual Freedom* 28 (1979):25ff.

8. E. Edmund Reutter, Jr., "Censorship in Public Schools: Some Recent Legal Developments," in *Current Legal Issues in Education,* ed. M. A. McGhehey (Topeka, Kans.: National Organization on Legal Problems of Education, 1977).

9. American Association of School Librarians, *"Policies and Procedures for Selection of Instructional Materials,"* (Chicago: AASL, 1976); National Council for the Social Studies, *Academic Freedom* (Washington, D.C.: NCSS, 1971).

10. Kunder, *op. cit.*

11. American Association of School Administrators, Association for Supervision and Curriculum Development, National Association of Elementary School Principals, and National Association of Secondary School Principals, *Censorship: The Challenge to Freedom in the Schools* (Washington, D.C.: AASA, ASCD, NAEP, NASSP, 1975).

CHAPTER 2   Bibliography

Davis, James E. ed. *Dealing with Censorship.* Urbana, Ill.: National Council of Teachers of English, 1979.

Educational Products Information Exchange. *Improving Materials Selection Procedures: A Basic "How To" Handbook.* Report No. 54. New York City: EPIE, 1973.

Educational Research Service. *The New Copyright Law and Education.* Arlington, Va.: ERS, 1977.

Joint Project of American Library Association, National Council of Teachers of English, and National Education Association. *The New Copyright Law: Questions Teachers and Librarians Ask.* 1977. (This handbook may be purchased from any of the project sponsors, e.g., American Library Association, 50 E. Huron Street, Chicago, Ill., 60611).

Maxson, Marilyn M., and Kraus, Larry L. "Curriculum Censorship in the Public School." *The Educational Forum* 43 (1979):393–407.

Miller, Jerome K. *Applying the New Copyright Law: A Guide for Educators and Librarians.* Chicago: American Library Association, 1979.

Troost, F. William. "Copyright Today: An Interesting Paradox." *Audiovisual Instruction* 24, (1979):4–5.

Woods, L. B. "Is Academic Freedom Dead in Public Schools?" *Phi Delta Kappan* 61 (1979):104–106.

3 *Access to Curriculum Materials*

Thousands of curriculum materials are available, yet many educators have trouble locating specific materials that relate to their instructional needs. This chapter describes the wide range of catalogs and services that can help you obtain information about curriculum materials, and explains how to use the corresponding inventory of catalogs presented in Appendix C.

Access refers to the process that educators use to search for and locate materials relating to a particular topic or need. For example, a teacher who conducts a search for social studies materials to use with low-reading-skill students is engaged in the process of access.

The process of accessing curriculum materials is often unplanned and incidental to other activities. Educators generally become aware of available materials in the casual process of talking with colleagues, reading professional journals, and attending conventions. Publishers' representatives visit school districts occasionally to display their companies' wares.

Although these activities help educators stay abreast of available materials, they are deficient in at least two respects. First, no matter how up-to-date an educator may be, it is virtually impossible to be aware of *all* that is available. The second problem is that even when the educator is aware of a particular set of curriculum materials, he or she may lack essential information (e.g., author's name, publisher's address) for accessing them.

These problems with traditional access procedures indicate the need for educators to become more systematic and active in search activities. Fortunately, systematic searches are more possible now because of the many curriculum materials catalogs that have been developed in recent years. These catalogs usually consist of lists of curriculum materials, organized by subject area. Each set of materials on the list is accompanied by basic descriptive information, for example, author, publisher, date of publication, cost, grade level suitability. Some catalogs also provide evaluations of the materials, a handy feature because it helps educators decide which materials are most appropriate without the bother of ordering them for inspection.

The use of curriculum materials catalogs is not without problems. First, the great number of catalogs — perhaps 200 or more — can easily overwhelm an educator faced with the task of selecting materials. Another problem is the inevitable problem of catalogs providing inaccurate and out-of-date information, or failing to include recently published materials.

Curriculum materials catalogs typically are published as hardbound or softbound books and pamphlets. Curriculum materials bibliographies in the

ERIC system (described a bit later) are available in microfiche or photocopy format.

The most sophisticated catalogs are computerized and allow the user to search for curriculum materials by topic and by student characteristics. For example, the catalogs of the National Information Center for Educational Media (NICEM) and of the National Information Center for Special Education Materials (NICSEM) are available in book format and on computer tape. (These catalogs are items 11–18 and 87–88 in Appendix C.) Computerized catalogs have three potential advantages over traditional catalog formats: speed of use by the educator; easy updating by the catalog compiler; and capability for specialized searches that involve the intersection of several descriptors, for example, a search for all (1) math materials (2) at the elementary level (3) in an audiovisual format (4) for slow learners.

Inventory of Curriculum Materials Catalogs

Catalogs of Catalogs

There are three types of curriculum materials catalogs. First, "catalogs of catalogs" help you obtain access to the great many catalogs of curriculum materials. In other words, the catalogs of catalogs do not contain listings of curriculum *materials*; instead, they contain listings of curriculum materials *catalogs*.

A very useful catalog of this type is *Selecting Instructional Media* (1) compiled by Mary Robinson Sive. This book lists hundreds of comprehensive catalogs, subject-specific catalogs (e.g., bilingual education, career education), and catalogs organized by media (e.g., audio recordings, filmloops). Sive includes the following information about each catalog:

- author and publisher
- purpose
- grade level
- organization of the catalog
- subject headings and media represented
- number of entries
- period covered; revision and updating
- producers represented

Selecting Instructional Media is an invaluable source of information for systematically selecting curriculum materials. You should note that it does not include catalogs of *print* materials.

Curriculum-General Catalogs

The second type of catalog is the curriculum-general catalog that lists materials across a broad spectrum of curriculum subject areas. Most of them restrict their coverage in some way, however. For example, some curriculum-general catalogs list only 16mm films. Others limit their listings to free or inexpensive materials.

Curriculum-Specific Catalogs

The third type of catalog is the curriculum-specific catalog. These catalogs specialize in a particular subject area, for example, reading, bilingual education, social studies. The curriculum-specific catalog is the most common format for organizing and listing the many thousands of educational materials available today.

Organization of the Inventory

This book includes an inventory of catalogs of curriculum materials (Appendix C). The inventory provides a list of the catalogs that I believe are most available and helpful to educators, and gives a good idea of the wide range of curriculum materials catalogs available.

Several criteria were used to compile the inventory of catalogs. The first criterion is how recently the catalog was published and how current is its information about curriculum materials. With a few exceptions, no catalogs published prior to 1975 are included in the inventory. Another criterion for inclusion is the amount of information provided about each product listed in the catalog. Catalogs that contain evaluations of materials were preferred to catalogs that only present descriptive data. The third criterion is ready availability of the catalog for purchase. Finally, only catalogs of American-published materials were considered for inclusion.

Education journals were not included in the inventory in order to keep its size manageable. However, you should be aware that many education journals publish listings and reviews of new materials. A good index to education journals is *Guide to Periodicals in Education and Its Academic Disciplines, Second Edition* (2).

The inventory in the appendix includes 96 catalogs organized under the following headings:

1. General Catalogs (ref. nos. 1–10)
2. General Catalogs: Nonprint Media (ref. nos. 11–19)

3. General Catalogs: Specific Age or Grade Levels (ref. nos. 20–31)
4. The Arts (ref. nos. 32–33)
5. Bilingual and Multicultural Education (ref. nos. 34–40)
6. Career and Consumer Education (ref. nos. 41–44)
7. English, Language Arts, and Reading (ref. nos. 45–49)
8. Foreign Languages (ref. nos. 50–52)
9. Mathematics and Science (ref. nos. 53–58)
10. Mental Health, Physical Health, Recreation, Religion, and Safety (ref. nos. 59–68)
11. Social Studies (ref. nos. 69–86)
12. Special Education: Handicapped and Gifted (ref. nos. 87–90)
13. Vocational and Technical Education (ref. nos. 91–96)

Each of the 96 catalogs is accompanied by the following information:

- cost of the catalog
- grade levels for which the materials in the catalog are intended
- number of materials listed in the catalog
- publication data
- address from which the catalog can be ordered.

Before ordering a particular catalog for your use, you might check whether it is available locally. Many colleges and universities, and most school districts, maintain curriculum libraries, usually located in the reference section.

Publishers of Catalogs

Several organizations and publishers are worthy of special note because of their extensive involvement in assisting educators to access curriculum materials. The *Educational Products Information Exchange (EPIE)* is generally well known to educators. It was established in 1967 to provide something comparable to Consumer's Union (publishers of *Consumer Reports*) for educational materials and products. Annual membership in EPIE entitles one to receive eight issues of *EPIE Reports* and eighteen issues of the newsletter *EPIEgram*. Many of the Reports are compilations and analyses of curriculum materials in specific subject areas. Some of them are included among the catalogs (e.g., number 28) in Appendix B.

In addition to its publications, EPIE provides programs to train teachers to select appropriate curriculum materials. EPIE currently is involved in developing a national network and computer index to media materials. Called the *EPIE Nonprint Instructional Materials Project*, it is being designed to help educators achieve quick access to information about curriculum materials.

The *National Information Center for Educational Media*, located at the University of Southern California, has published a variety of curriculum materials catalogs. Each catalog provides an index to a specific media format, for example, overhead transparencies. These catalogs are described in entries 11 through 18 of Appendix B. The *National Information Center for Special Education Materials* is also located at the University of Southern California. Its catalogs are described in entry 88 of the inventory.

The *Educational Resources Information Center (ERIC)* is a government-funded clearinghouse for all types of education documents, including catalogs of curriculum materials. The documents are abstracted and indexed in a monthly publication *Resources in Education (RIE)*. Each document is given an identification number, for example, ED 654 321. If an educator wishes to obtain the document after reading the abstract in RIE, he or she can order it from ERIC in microfiche or regular print format. Some education libraries maintain collections of ERIC documents in microfiche format. Several of the catalogs in Appendix B (e.g., number 83) are available from the original developer or from ERIC.

The *National Diffusion Network* (NDN) was established by the U.S. Office of Education to promote the dissemination of exemplary programs. This dissemination agency links successful projects developed by local school systems with other school systems which might benefit from them. Before a project is accepted for dissemination by the NDN, it must be deemed exemplary by a group called the Joint Dissemination Review Panel. This panel accepts projects for dissemination if they are replicable at other school sites and if their demonstrated effectiveness is educationally significant. One of the services provided by NDN to educators is catalogs of approved projects (for example, Catalog 3 in Appendix C).

CHAPTER 3 Notes

1. Mary Robinson Sive, *Selecting Instructional Media* (Littleton, Colo.: Libraries Unlimited, 1978).

2. William L. Camp and Bryan L. Schwark, *Guide to Periodicals in Education and Its Academic Disciplines,* 2nd edition (Metuchen, N.J.: Scarecrow, 1975).

CHAPTER 3   Bibliography

Bain, Helen P., and Groseclose, J. Ronald. "The Dissemination Dilemma and a Plan for Uniting Disseminators and Practitioners." *Phi Delta Kappan* 61 (1979):101–103.

Gall, Meredith D. "Competency-based Teacher Education Materials: How Available? How Usable? How Effective?" *Journal of Teacher Education* 30 (1979): 58–61.

Simmons, Beatrice T., and Carter, Yvonne B. *Aids to Media Selection for Students and Teachers.* Washington, D.C.: U.S. Office of Education, Bureau of Elementary and Secondary Education, Office of Libraries & Learning Resources, 1979.

4 *Analysis of Curriculum Materials*

A mistake sometimes made in curriculum materials selection is to judge a set of materials before their purpose and organization are properly understood. This chapter stresses the importance of carefully describing the salient features of curriculum products before evaluating them and making an adoption decision. Also included is an inventory of 39 descriptive features of curriculum materials, divided into four sections: publication and cost information; physical properties; content; and instructional properties.

The Need for an Analytic Framework

Educators sometimes make the mistake of judging a set of curriculum materials before understanding what the materials are and how they work. The recommended procedure is first to access an array of curriculum materials. Next, each set of materials should be *analyzed* accurately and in detail. The resulting analyses provide the basis for making sound judgments about each product's quality and appropriateness for a particular instructional situation. The judgmental process (called "appraisal" here) is described in Chapter 6. This chapter and Chapter 5 deal with the analytic process.

Analysis is the process of separating a whole into its component parts and examining the parts by themselves and in relation to each other. To understand how analysis applies to the selection of curriculum materials, consider what happens as we inspect new curriculum materials for the first time, for example, a textbook series. As we pick up the materials, we first look at them as a whole, and in so doing, classify them as textbooks. Then we notice such details as the title, author, and publisher. The type of cover (hardbound or soft cover) might attract our attention. As we flip through the pages of one of the books in the series, we see the publication date, intended grade level, presence of pictures interspersed with text, use of color, number of pages. In studying the Table of Contents, we obtain some idea about the topics covered in the text, and the emphasis placed on each topic. The introduction may tell us something about the author's philosophy and approach in writing the textbook. As we proceed still further in our analysis, we might ask ourselves whether supplementary materials, such as an instructor's guide, are available, and whether the publisher provides in-service workshops to help teachers use the materials properly.

The preceding example demonstrates that analysis is important for developing an understanding of curriculum materials. In current practice, only a few features of materials are noted in making selection decisions. Superficial features might receive considerable attention (e.g., cost, durability), whereas the materials' instructional properties (e.g., provision for individualization of instruction) may be overlooked completely. Therefore, educators need to be aware of the entire range of curriculum material features that can be analyzed. Most important, they should decide on an analytic framework *before* inspection of the materials begins. An analytic framework is simply an organized list of features to be described for each set of curriculum materials accessed.

Inventory of Dimensions for Analyzing Curriculum Materials

The following is a comprehensive list of 39 features that characterize curriculum materials. Each feature represents a dimension, such as cost, on which different curriculum materials can be compared. You are invited to use the descriptive labels provided in the inventory or to invent your own.

The dimensions of the inventory have been organized into four categories: (1) publication and cost information; (2) physical properties of materials; (3) content of materials; and (4) instructional properties of materials. No hierarchy of relative importance should be implied from this order of presentation, however. Table 1 provides a summary of the inventory.

Each dimension in the inventory is given a descriptive label and explained if necessary. Procedures for observing the dimension are stated, if appropriate. Also, a series of questions are provided to help you critically examine curriculum materials with respect to each dimension. Your own personal, critical examination is important as a check on the accuracy and completeness of information provided by publishers and other sources. Some of the questions may seem too obvious to merit inclusion but are included here so that the list is comprehensive.

Publication and Cost Information

The first set of dimensions for analyzing curriculum materials involves cost and publication history. Information about these dimensions is sometimes included in the materials themselves (e.g., names of authors) or is provided by publishers in their advertising literature. Publishers' representatives are another source of information. Catalogs of curriculum materials (see Chapter Three) usually contain some information about cost and publication history.

Publishers may provide certain information about their materials, but may not include other information which could influence an adoption decision. For example, a publisher may provide many cost details about a particular set of materials they wish you to purchase, but fail to inform you that they shortly will be replaced with a new edition. Or you may receive information about how to purchase a curriculum product (e.g., an instructional game), but no information about whether replacement parts are available and their cost.

TABLE 1 Inventory of Dimensions for Analyzing Curriculum Materials

Publication and Cost

1. Authors
2. Cost
3. Development history
4. Edition
5. Publication date
6. Publisher
7. Purchase procedures
8. Quantity
9. Special requirements
10. Teacher training

Physical Properties

11. Aesthetic Appeal
12. Components
13. Consumables
14. Durability
15. Media format
16. Quality
17. Safety

Content

18. Approach
19. Instructional objectives
20. Instructional objectives — types
21. Issues orientation
22. Multiculturalism
23. Scope and sequence
24. Sex roles
25. Time-boundedness

Instructional Properties

26. Assessment devices
27. Comprehensibility
28. Coordination with the curriculum
29. Individualization
30. Instructional effectiveness
31. Instructional patterns
32. Learner characteristics
33. Length
34. Management system
35. Motivational properties
36. Prerequisites
37. Readability
38. Role of student
39. Role of teacher

These examples demonstrate the need to specify the date of publication and cost information about curriculum materials. If you simply rely on information provided by the publisher, you may encounter problems in purchasing and using the materials. The following list of dimensions includes questions that you may wish to ask before seeking cost and publication information.

A final bit of advice: Since publishers' representatives inadvertently make errors in quoting cost figures, you are advised to ask for official cost lists from the publisher.

1. Authors   *The persons responsible for the development and writing of the materials.*

Large-scale curriculum projects may have a senior editor, who supervises a writing team.

- Who are the authors of the materials?
- What is the institutional affiliation of the authors?
- What is its reputation?
- What is the professional background of the authors?
- In the case of multiple authorship, what was the role of each author in developing the materials?

2. Cost   *The price that is paid for obtaining the materials from the publishers.*

The cost for a particular set of materials may vary depending upon the conditions of purchase and the components involved.

- Is purchase the only option? Can materials (especially, films) be rented? Can rental fees be applied to the cost of purchase?
- What is the cost of each component (e.g., textbook, instructor's guide, student workbook) in the set of materials?
- Is there a shipping charge for the materials? Sales tax?
- Is the cost per unit discounted if you order multiple copies? If you send immediate payment?
- Is the cost guaranteed for a particular period of time? Are price increases likely?
- Are less expensive versions of the materials available (e.g., hard cover versus soft cover textbooks)?
- What is the cost of replacement parts (e.g., individual items in a simulation game)?
- What is the cost of installation and in-service training, if available?
- Are there "hidden" costs, such as the need for additional resources or facilities required to use the materials?
- How fast can the materials be sent to you after the order has been placed?

3. Development History   *The process and events that occurred in the development and production of the materials.*

Information about development history sometimes yields insights into the nature and purpose of the materials.

- How was the development of the materials funded?
- Did significant problems or events occur during the development of the materials?
- How long was the period of development?

4. Edition *The version of the curriculum materials that is to be purchased.*

The first edition refers to the first publication of the materials. Subsequent revisions of the materials' content are numbered serially, e.g., second edition, third edition. Two editions of a set of curriculum materials can be issued at the same time, with variations: in design (e.g., an edition for regular sighted students and an edition for visually impaired children); in content (e.g., an edition for low-reading-skill students and an edition for high-reading-skill students); and in language (e.g., an English language edition and a translation into French). The edition number or name is usually printed at the front of the materials.

- Is there more than one edition of the materials available for purchase?
- Is a new edition (revision) of the materials to be published in the near future?
- How does the current edition differ from earlier editions?
- If a new edition is to be published, will copies of the earlier materials still be available?

5. Publication Date *The date on which the materials are printed or made available for sale.*

In the case of books and audiovisual materials, only the year is indicated. In the case of newspapers, magazines, and journals, the month and day also may be indicated.

- For materials not yet released, how reliable is the publisher's anticipated date of publication?
- In the case of newspapers, magazines, and journals, how often are they published?

6. Publisher *The organization that produces and sells the materials.*

Some materials are produced by one organization, and offered for sale by another organization. The production organization is usually called the publisher, and the sales organization is called the distributor. Many free and inexpensive materials are published by business and industry.

- Is more than one organization involved in the production and sale of the materials?
- What is the official name and address of the publisher?
- If the publisher has more than one location, what is the address of the main office and of branch offices?
- What types of materials are produced by the publisher?
- Does the publisher have an established reputation?
- Is the publisher owned by another company?
- Do industry-provided materials "advertise" the products of a particular company (1)?

7. Purchase Procedures   *The process of ordering materials from the publisher.*

Some materials must be ordered from a warehouse address that is different from the publisher's address. Some publishers have sales representatives from whom the materials can be ordered.

- What is the address from which materials are ordered?
- How is payment for the materials to be made?
- If problems occur in ordering or receiving materials, who can be contacted?
- Must the billing order be paid immediately, or is there a specified payment period?

8. Quantity   *The number of copies of each component in a set of curriculum materials.*

Some curriculum packages provide multiple copies of one or more components for classroom use.

- Does the set of materials contain a sufficient quantity of each component for the anticipated enrollment?
- If a sufficient quantity is not provided, can additional copies be ordered?
- Does the publisher give permission for the purchaser to reproduce extra copies of components?

9. Special Requirements

Staff, equipment, or facilities not provided by the publisher and not ordinarily found in classrooms.

Some curriculum materials are not self-contained. For example, filmstrip loops in a curriculum kit require a projector for viewing. Spirit masters require that multiple copies be made on a duplicating machine. A science kit may describe experiments, but not provide all of the materials needed to conduct the experiments.

- Does the school need to purchase or otherwise obtain additional materials in order to implement the curriculum package?
- Do the materials impose special space or staff requirements?
- Is the special equipment or material available directly from the publisher?
- Does the publisher require that the school district purchase consultant time or in-service training before the materials can be installed?

10. Teacher Training

The extent to which teachers require special training in order to use the materials properly.

Some publishers include workshops for teachers as a service when their curriculum materials are purchased by a school.

- Is teacher training an extra cost, or is it included with the purchase of the materials?
- Is the training directly relevant to the skills that teachers will need to use the materials effectively?

Physical Properties of the Materials

The second set of dimensions for analyzing curriculum materials concerns their physical construction. How many physical *components* make up the curriculum product? How *durable* are the materials? How *safe*? What is the *quality* of the materials used in the construction of the product? These are physical properties of the materials that can be analyzed and described.

Knowledge about the physical properties of materials is obviously an important factor in making adoption decisions. No one would wish to buy curriculum materials such as educational toys and science experiments that are unsafe for students to use. Durability and quality are important factors to consider in determining whether the cost of the materials is fair. A high purchase price might be justified if the materials are of high quality, durable, and reusable by successive classes of students.

Some information about the physical properties of curriculum materials can be obtained from the publisher, but most of it will come from your own inspection and judgment of the materials. For example, you will need to rely on your experience in determining whether the materials will hold up under the type of wear to which they will be subjected by your students. Judgments about quality of materials may require technical expertise. Media specialists will be especially helpful in this phase of curriculum materials analysis.

11. Aesthetic Appeal   *The extent to which the materials are pleasing or beautiful in appearance.*

Some materials offend the eye, ear, or other sense. Others have been constructed so that they have aesthetic appeal.

- Are any aspects of the materials unusually attractive, plain, or crude?

12. Components   *Each separate piece in a set of curriculum materials.*

Many materials consist of a single item, such as textbook or film. However, other materials may include several items, e.g., a textbook with accompanying instructor's manual, student workbook, and supplemental enrichment booklets. Care must be taken in determining all of the components, required or optional, in using the materials. In the case of materials such as instructional games, each and every piece of the game should be labelled as a separate component. A list of components is helpful in checking completeness of a set of materials when received from the publisher or after they have been used in class.

- Does the publisher provide a list of the package's components?
- Must all of the components in a curriculum package be purchased? Are some optional?
- Does the publisher use distinctive labels or descriptors to refer to components of materials?

13. Consum-ables *Materials that are designed to be used by only one student or group of students.*

The most common type of consumables is workbooks in which students write their answers.

- Is it possible to redesign consumable materials so that they can be reused?

14. Durability *The extent to which the materials will hold up under conditions of use.*

The binding and cover (especially, paperback covers) of textbooks and other print materials are likely to deteriorate with heavy use. Other materials may have components vulnerable to wear.

- Does the publisher offer any guarantees or assurances concerning durability?
- Can the materials be repaired if they become worn?

15. Media format *A description of the components of curriculum materials that enables one to infer the medium used, e.g., print, audio, video, graphic, mechanical object.*

One may wish to state explicitly the media format of each component in the curriculum package.

- Is more than one medium utilized in the curriculum package?
- Does the publisher or developer provide a rationale for using a particular medium to achieve an instructional goal?

16. Quality *The fineness of the materials used to construct the curriculum package.*

Materials (e.g., paper, book bindings, pictures in a book, film stock, sound reproduction on audio casettes) differ in quality. Better quality materials are usually more expensive than low quality materials, although this is not necessarily the case.

- Are the materials used in the construction of the curriculum product unusually high or low in quality?
- In the case of printed materials, does the paper produce a glare?

17. Safety   *The extent to which the materials do not pose a hazard to the physical and emotional wellbeing of students.*

Some materials, especially toys and games used in early childhood education, and supplies used in science classes (e.g., chemicals) may pose a hazard if used improperly.

- Does the publisher state any precautions that should be followed in using the materials?
- In the case of toys and games, have they been certified as safe by a consumer protection agency?
- Do the materials contain content that may cause an emotional upset in some students?

Content of Materials

Many educators view content as the key dimension of curriculum materials. In their view, the content *is* the curriculum. Content consists of the facts, concepts, generalizations, skills, and attitudes contained in the materials.

Curriculum content sometimes is analyzed and stated in terms of the materials' instructional or behavioral objectives. Another approach is to analyze and describe content in terms of scope and sequence. Also, educators may have a special interest in certain aspects of the materials' content, for example, the manner in which different ethnic groups are represented.

Contemporary curriculum developers are likely to include lists of objectives or a scope and sequence in their materials, or both. Even if all of these are available, you are advised to do your own careful study to determine what knowledge, skills, and attitudes are actually conveyed by the materials. The Table of Contents and headings in the text can be used to obtain a quick overview of content coverage.

18. Approach   *The particular philosophy, values, and biases that guided the development of the materials.*

Two sets of curriculum materials may cover the same content, but differ in approach. For example, one developer may view the learner's task as "knowing" the content in the sense of being able to recall it when asked to do so. The other developer may use an inquiry approach in which students are encouraged to use the content as a springboard for making their own discoveries.

- Is the developer's approach explicitly stated in the introduction to the materials?
- Is the developer's approach consistent with the curriculum philosophy of the school district?
- Is there anything about the developer's approach that is likely to be controversial?

19. Instructional Objectives

The learning outcomes that the materials are designed to achieve.

Some curriculum experts believe that this is the most important aspect of materials analysis.

- Are the objectives stated in behavioral form?
- Are the objectives explicitly stated, or must they be inferred?
- Is there reason to think that the materials might have objectives not stated by the developer?

20. Instructional Objectives — Types

The classification of instructional objectives, usually into the categories of cognition, affect, and psychomotor.

The taxonomies developed by Benjamin Bloom and his colleagues are often used for this purpose (2). A distinction made by some curriculum developers is to classify instructional objectives into lower cognitive and higher cognitive categories.

- Have the objectives of the materials been classified by the developers or by some other group?

21. Issues Orientation

The extent to which the curriculum content reflects the uncertainty of knowledge.

Some curriculum materials present content as a set of facts to be learned. Other materials express a sensitivity to the uncertainty that underlies much of what we claim to know. Or the curriculum content may include contrasting views of different groups on particular issues (for example, the Biblical versus the scientific explanation of creation and evolution).

- Are issues explicitly stated? Is evidence for and against each side of the issue presented?
- Are alternative interpretations of events and artistic productions presented?
- Do the materials contain questions designed to stimulate students to think productively about what they have read or seen or done?

**22. Multicul-
turalism**   *The extent to which the content of the materials reflects the perspectives and contributions of a variety of cultural and ethnic groups.*

Some curriculum materials, in their choice of content, express a limited cultural point of view. Other materials are designed with a sensitivity to multicultural aspects of the curriculum content, and a sensitivity to the fact that students from different cultural backgrounds may learn differently.

- Do the developers state an awareness of multiculturalism in the design of their materials?
- Are specific cultural and ethnic groups referred to in the materials? How often? In positive, negative, or neutral ways?

**23. Scope and
Sequence**   *The range of topics covered in a set of curriculum materials, and the order in which they are presented.*

The developer of the materials sometimes includes a chart organizing the curriculum content in terms of scope and sequence.

- Is scope and sequence explicitly stated by the materials developer? If not, can they be inferred from the table of contents or from other information in the materials?
- Is a rationale for the scope and sequence provided?

24. Sex Roles   *The delineation of male and female roles in the content of the materials.*

Much of the school curriculum involves people, and one of the most salient characteristics of people is their gender. In portraying people, curriculum developers intentionally or unwittingly take a position about what is appropriate and inappropriate sex role behavior.

- If the content deals with people, are persons of both sexes represented equally in all respects — for example, in frequency of appearance as a main character, as an active or passive participant, and as workers in different occupational roles?

- Are the persons in the curriculum content portrayed in terms of stereotypic sex roles?

25. Time-Bounded-ness

The extent to which the materials reflect a particular point in time.

Some curriculum materials are quickly dated. For example, a film may depict styles of dress, language, and possessions (e.g., automobiles) that are no longer current. Other materials are less timebound, for example, math curriculum materials. Date of publication provides some clue about whether the materials are outdated but delays in production may result in a recent publication date, even though the materials were developed several years earlier.

- Is time-boundedness a relevant dimension for analyzing the content of the materials?
- Is there anything about the curriculum content or style of presentation that suggests the materials are out of date, that is, not reflecting current culture and state of knowledge?

Instructional Properties of Materials

Analysis of the instructional properties of curriculum materials is not easy. It requires, first of all, that you determine the instructional design or pattern of the materials. This means an examination of the sequence of activities which students and the teacher follow as they work their way through the materials.

Analysis of instructional properties also should include an attempt to determine how and why the sequence of prescribed activities brings about the intended learning outcomes. For example, instruction in a new skill (e.g., two-place addition) sometimes follows this pattern: presentation of a model showing how the skill is used; practice examples for students to use; and an answer key so that students can check their solutions. Research has demonstrated that this sequence is effective in developing skills (3). However, it may not be effective or appropriate for other types of learning outcomes, such as the development of attitudes. The next chapter presents examples of instructional patterns and techniques for detecting them.

Certain properties of materials may have special instructional value, that is, they affect students' learning of content in the materials. Comprehensibility, length of instruction required by the materials, and presence of motivational techniques are examples of instructional properties that probably affect learning. Readability, as one type of comprehensibility, is sufficiently important that it is discussed further in the next chapter.

26. Assessment Devices
Measures of student learning outcomes that are included in the curriculum package.

Assessment devices take a variety of forms, for example, multiple-choice tests, short answer tests, essays. Assessment devices can be used to measure progress while the student is learning the curriculum content or can be used to measure the student's final (e.g., end of course) level of learning. Some tests are intended for teacher administration; others are self-testing devices for the student's own use.

- Do the materials contain a variety of assessment devices?
- Are answer keys provided?
- Are test items related directly to the instructional objectives of the materials?
- Do the materials provide more than one version of each assessment device?
- Are test norms or standards of performance presented?

27. Comprehensibility (Clarity)
The extent to which the learner is able to understand the content of the materials.

If the presentation of content is poorly organized or has difficult vocabulary, the reader will have difficulty in learning from the materials. The comprehensibility factor interacts with learner characteristics — a particular set of materials may be incomprehensible to one learner, but not to another. Since most curriculum content is in written form, comprehensibility of text (see dimension 37 — readability) is a particularly important aspect of materials analysis. Comprehensibility is not limited to text, but applies to graphics and artwork as well.

- Do the developers or publishers present evidence that the materials will be comprehensible to the students for whom they are intended?
- If the publisher presents readability data, what formulas or techniques were used to generate them?

28. Coordination with the Curriculum
The extent to which a particular set of materials needs to be considered in relation to other materials or the more general curriculum.

Some curriculum materials are designed to be used in conjunction with other materials, an integrated math-science curriculum, for example. Curriculum materials also may be designed to be used in a certain type of school or class environment — for example, classrooms with activity centers, open classrooms, alternative schools.

- Are the materials compatible with other materials and the general curriculum in the setting in which they will be used?

- If the materials are designed for use at a certain grade level, must they be coordinated with the instruction that students receive at lower or higher grade levels?

29. Individualization
The extent to which the curriculum materials are designed so that they can be used differently with different learners.

Self-pacing, alternative activities, and content geared to different interests are the most common ways in which materials are individualized.

- What are the specific ways in which the materials can be individualized?

- If the materials are individualized, will this pose any special management problems for the teacher?

30. Instructional Effectiveness
The extent to which there is evidence documenting the effectiveness of the materials.

Developers of federally or state funded curriculum packages are likely to collect evaluation data as part of their development effort. These data may be compiled into technical reports, which are available upon request from the developer or publisher.

- If technical reports are available, do they provide data demonstrating that students learn from the materials? Do they contain data on teacher and student satisfaction in using the materials?

- Have other districts purchased the materials, and can they be contacted to discuss their results with the materials?

31. Instruc-
tional
Patterns

The form and sequence of instructional activities in a particular set of materials.

The form and sequence should have a rationale showing how they help the student achieve the curriculum package's objectives. Even in complex packages, the design is usually built around one or two repetitive instructional patterns. The analysis of instructional patterns is discussed further in the next chapter.

- What type of instructional pattern is incorporated in the materials?
- What is the rationale for the instructional pattern?

32. Learner
Character-
istics

The characteristics of learners for whom the materials are appropriate.

Learners vary significantly in aptitude, motivational level, prior learning history, handicaps, interests, and skill level (especially reading skill). Developers sometimes orient their materials to learners who have similar ability in one or more of these areas. Some materials contain options so that they can be individualized for different types of learners. Learner characteristics are discussed further in the next chapter.

- Have the materials been developed for a specific type of learner?
- Are there types of learners who may experience difficulty in using the materials?

33. Length

The amount of instructional time needed to complete the activities in a set of curriculum materials.

The length of some materials can be measured by a simple quantitative index, such as, number of pages in a book or viewing time for a film. More difficult to measure is *instructional length*, the amount of time required by learners to achieve the materials' instructional objectives.

- Does the developer or publisher provide guidelines on the length of time needed by students to work through the materials?
- Are there optional activities that can be used to lengthen instruction, or deleted to shorten it?

34. Management System

Procedures to monitor and control the use of curriculum materials.

Complex curriculum packages sometimes include procedures to help teachers track students' progress through the materials. Some sophisticated management systems are computerized to give teachers daily readouts of how many units in the materials each student has mastered.

- Do the materials include charts and other record-keeping devices to help the teacher track students' progress with the materials?
- Are diagnostic-prescriptive aids provided to help the teacher pinpoint and remediate individual student difficulties in mastering the curriculum materials' content?

35. Motivational Properties

The extent to which the curriculum materials contain elements particularly designed to attract and maintain the learner's attention.

Certain instructional techniques are commonly thought to motivate the learner — a flashy introduction, surprises, questions embedded in the materials, content relevant to the learner's interests, application of the content to situations that the learner might encounter in the "real" world.

- Are the materials likely to motivate students?
- Do the materials contain motivational techniques to excite and maintain teachers' interest in using them?

36. Prerequisites

The extent to which certain prior learnings must be achieved before the curriculum materials can be used effectively.

The usual prerequisite is a certain level of skill or knowledge of content. Prerequisites are usually specified so that students need not struggle with a body of curriculum content before they are ready.

- Are prerequisites clearly specified by the developer, or can they be inferred from examining the materials?
- If students have not acquired the prerequisite knowledge, skill, etc., can they still use the materials while receiving supplementary assistance?

**37. Read-
ability**

*The extent to which the prose content of curriculum materials is compre-
hensible to the reader.*

Readability has been conceptualized and measured in different ways. (Readability is a particular type of comprehensibility — see dimension 27.) Sentence length, vocabulary, and complexity of sentence structure are factors
thought to determine whether a passage of prose is readable. Procedures for
measuring readability are discussed in the next chapter.

- Are the materials readable by the students for whom they are intended?

**38. Role of
Student**

*The activities in which students engage as they interact with the materials
and the teacher.*

Some materials call for relatively passive activity, e.g., reading a book, viewing a film. Other materials more actively engage the student, e.g., completing
a quiz immediately after viewing a film, playing an instructional game, par-
ticipating in a discussion after reading a story.

- What are the specific types of activities in which the materials engage
  the student?
- Do the materials engage the student in activities that are relevant to
  the materials' objectives?
- Do the materials provide a mix of relatively passive and active tasks?

**39. Role of
Teacher**

*The function of a teacher as he or she uses the curriculum materials in an
instructional situation.*

Some materials are self-contained and require very little teacher support.
Other materials require the teacher to use certain teaching methods to introduce new content or to rehearse and explain content presented in the materials.

- In using the materials, is the teacher's role more that of a manager or
  of an instructor?
- Do the materials require teachers to perform activities that are likely
  to be beyond their range of expertise?

CHAPTER 4 Notes

1. Concerns about industry-provided materials are well-documented in: Sheila Harty, *Hucksters in the Classroom: A Review of Industry Propaganda in Schools* (Washington, D.C.: Center for Study of Responsive Law, 1979).

2. Benjamin S. Bloom, ed., *Taxonomy of Educational Objectives: Handbook 1: Cognitive Domain* (New York: David McKay, 1956).

3. Robert Gagné and Leslie Briggs, *Principles of Instructional Design*, 2nd ed. (New York: Holt, Rinehart and Winston, 1979).

5   *Additional Procedures for Analyzing Curriculum Materials*

The preceding chapter demonstrated that analysis of curriculum materials is a complex process that, carried out properly, can lead to a sound understanding of a particular curriculum product. Three dimensions of analysis are singled out for further discussion here: instructional patterns, readability, and match of learner characteristics with curriculum materials. Various forms for recording analyses of materials are also presented.

Curriculum Materials Analysis Forms

You are invited to modify the 39 dimensions of the inventory described in the preceding chapter to create your own form for analyzing materials, by rearranging, omitting, or inventing dimensions. Table 2 presents an example of how the descriptors can be adapted to create a curriculum materials analysis form. Note that more emphasis is placed on content and instructional dimensions than on publication, cost, and physical dimensions.

Analysis of Instructional Patterns

At some point in your inspection of curriculum materials you should ask, How do these materials work? How would I use them with my students? These questions are relevant to dimension 31 presented in the previous chapter, and can be answered by using the technique of instructional pattern analysis.

The purpose of instructional pattern analysis is to uncover the step-by-step pattern of activities that teacher and students follow in using a particular set of curriculum materials. This task is relatively brief because most materials — even complex curriculum packages — generally include no more than one or two different sequences.

A particular sequence tends to be repeated throughout. For example, suppose the first chapter of a textbook starts with an overview and glossary of key terms introduced in the chapter. Next follows the text of the chapter, with accompanying illustrations; the chapter concludes with a summary and a set of review questions. The same sequence probably will be followed in every chapter of the book. After analyzing and describing this sequence, you should possess a good understanding of the book's format and of how to use it in instruction.

Because instructional sequences tend to be used repetitively, it is not necessary to analyze the entire curriculum product. Even multigrade curriculum series generally are based on one or two instructional sequences

TABLE 2   Curriculum Materials Analysis Form

Publication and Cost

1. Title
2. Authors
3. Publisher
4. Publication Data and Edition
5. Cost
6. Other

Physical Properties

1. Components (Media)
2. Consumables
3. Durability
4. Quality
5. Other (e.g., Safety)

Content

1. Objectives
2. Scope and Sequence
3. Approach
4. Multiculturalism
5. Sex roles
6. Time-boundedness
7. Other

Instructional Properties

1. Instructional Pattern (Sequence of Activities)
2. Role of Student
3. Role of Teacher
4. Learner Characteristics
5. Readability (comprehensibility)
6. Prerequisites
7. Individualization
8. Length of Instruction
9. Motivational Features
10. Evidence of Effectiveness
11. Other

that are repeated within and across grade levels. Once you have "unlocked" the sequence, you can scan the other units in the materials to determine whether there are any significant departures from it.

In inspecting materials for instructional sequence patterns, you are advised to examine the preface, or teacher's guide, if available. These sources may explain the instructional sequence. Otherwise, you will need to determine the sequence on your own by using the following steps:

1. Determine the basic unit of instruction by which the content is organized. The units usually are called chapters, lessons, activities, or units.

2. Determine the sequence of activities incorporated in a sample unit, noting the roles required of students and teacher.

3. Check whether the sequence for the sample unit is repeated in other units.

4. Write a brief description of the sequence. A flow chart is useful for this purpose. A flow chart is simply a graphic display showing the sequence, or "flow," from one activity to the next (see Table 3).

As you become familiar with a variety of instructional sequence patterns across a range of curriculum materials, this analytic process will become increasingly easy to use.

An instructional sequence popularized by instructional technologists and training specialists is shown in Figure 4. The sequence begins with a review of the unit objectives by students and teacher. Next, the students take a pretest to determine what they already know about the objectives. If the student's performance on the pretest indicates mastery, he or she may proceed to the next unit or engage in enrichment activities. Otherwise, students proceed to receive instruction relevant to the unit objectives. The teacher may use preassessment data to determine special instructional needs of certain students.

The instructional phase may involve: (a) instruction by the teacher; (b) instruction mediated entirely by curriculum materials; or (c) a combination of the two. The sequence of activities within this phase may vary according to the nature of the unit objectives. For example, knowledge-type objectives may have a different sequence of activities than skill-type objectives.

Following instruction, students take a posttest to assess how well they have mastered the unit objectives. (The posttest may be the same as the pretest, or a paralled form of it.) If students have mastered the unit, they proceed to the next unit. Otherwise they "recycle" through another round of instruction and post-assessment. The second cycle of instruction probably will place more emphasis on remedial techniques and tutorial or small group teaching.

This type of instructional sequence is becoming increasingly common in curriculum materials. It is especially prevalent in curriculum materials intended for individualized instruction and diagnostic-prescriptive teaching. I view it as a generic model of instruction. Most curriculum materials follow some variation of this sequence. Variations usually occur in the addition or deletion of certain activities, and in the complexity of the instructional phase. Figures 5 and 6 present two examples of instructional sequence analysis; each represents a different type of curriculum product.

One advantage in analyzing a curriculum product's instructional sequence is that it helps you identify specific ways in which the product might be adapted to meet particular needs. For example, the steps of the sequence might be appropriate for your students, except that at one step they are expected to study some material beyond their reading level. Having pinpointed this problem, you can develop adaptations that preserve the general integrity of the sequence while also satisfying your special instructional requirements.

FIGURE 4

Instructional Sequence Commonly Used by Instructional Technologists

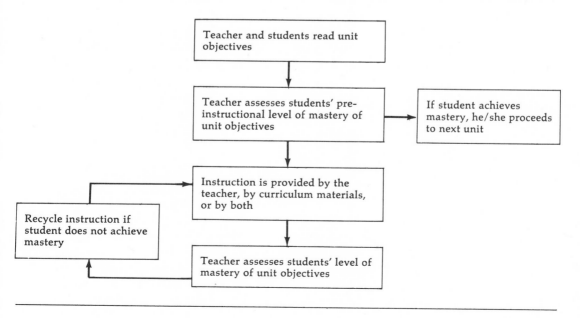

FIGURE 5 Instructional Sequence in Basic Reading Series

Title: S.R.A. Reading Program: Basic Reading Series.

Publisher: Science Research Associates.

Publication Date: 1970.

Materials: student readers and workbooks; teaching guides; workbook (teacher edition); placement tests; mastery tests; writing pads; spirit masters; word charts; satellites.

Purpose: to teach primary grade children the decoding skills, using the linguistic method.

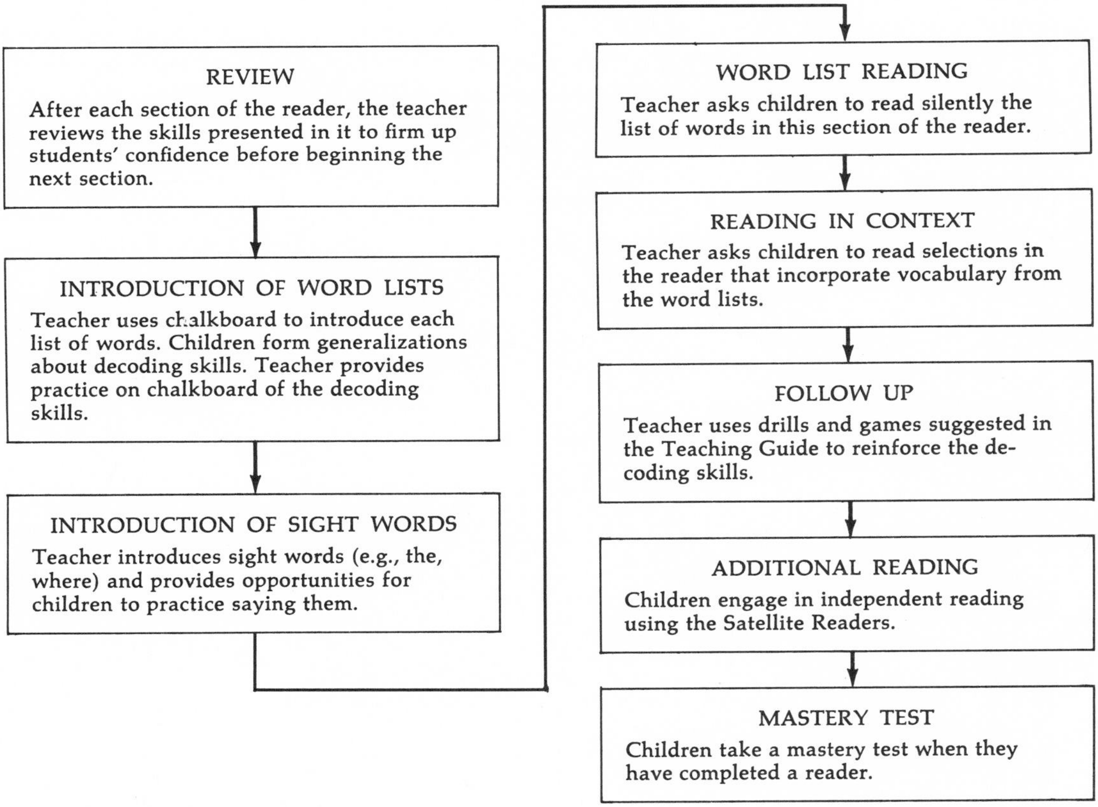

REVIEW

After each section of the reader, the teacher reviews the skills presented in it to firm up students' confidence before beginning the next section.

INTRODUCTION OF WORD LISTS

Teacher uses chalkboard to introduce each list of words. Children form generalizations about decoding skills. Teacher provides practice on chalkboard of the decoding skills.

INTRODUCTION OF SIGHT WORDS

Teacher introduces sight words (e.g., the, where) and provides opportunities for children to practice saying them.

WORD LIST READING

Teacher asks children to read silently the list of words in this section of the reader.

READING IN CONTEXT

Teacher asks children to read selections in the reader that incorporate vocabulary from the word lists.

FOLLOW UP

Teacher uses drills and games suggested in the Teaching Guide to reinforce the decoding skills.

ADDITIONAL READING

Children engage in independent reading using the Satellite Readers.

MASTERY TEST

Children take a mastery test when they have completed a reader.

Figure 6

Title: Discussing Controversial Issues

Publisher: Far West Laboratory for Educational Research and Development. (Distributed by Agency for Instructional Television.)

Publication Date: 1975

Materials: Four 16 mm. color films; teacher handbook; student handbook; coordinator handbook; student evaluation handbook.

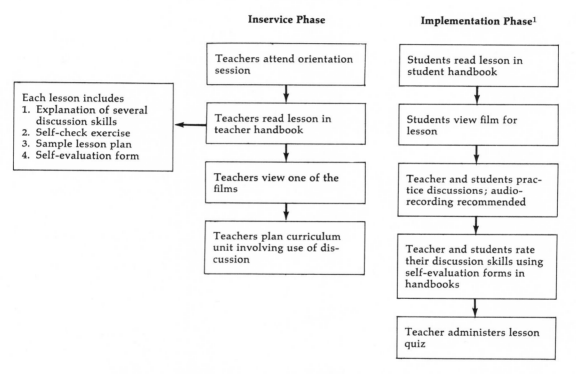

[1] This sequence of activities is followed for each of the four lessons in the training program.

Analysis of Readability

Students' learning and motivation will be impaired if they cannot read the text of their curriculum materials, yet they sometimes are assigned materials that are difficult or impossible for them to read. For example, an investigation of widely used K–6 materials in social studies found that the majority of them were one grade level or more above that recommended by the publisher (1). This problem can be alleviated if you evaluate the materials beforehand for readability.

Reading experts have developed many procedures for this purpose (2). I will describe four of them here. Two of the procedures for assessing readability require inspection of textual properties (e.g., sentence length); the other two procedures measure readability by having the teacher assess how students interact with the text.

INSPECTION PROCEDURES

The first procedure is the simplest: inspect samples of the text and judge their readability. If you are knowledgeable about how well students at different grade levels read, you can reasonably rate whether a set of materials will be read with good comprehension by the students. Personal ratings, while not infallible, do provide a quick check on publishers' claims about reading level. Teachers complain that publishers sometimes underestimate the readability of their materials.

A more sophisticated procedure involving inspection is to use a readability formula. More than thirty of these formulas have been developed; those developed by Flesch (3), Dale and Chall (4), McLaughlin (5), and Fry (6) are the most widely used. The formulas generally require selecting two or three short samples of prose from the text, and inspecting them for average sentence length, word length (number of syllables), and occurrence of infrequently used words.

The application of readability formulas can be illustrated by McLaughlin's SMOG index, which is the simplest of those listed above. The calculations are as follows:

1. Count 10 consecutive sentences near the beginning of the text; 10 sentences near the middle; and another 10 sentences near the end.

2. Count every word of 3 or more syllables in the 30 sentences selected in Step 1.

3. Determine the approximate square root of the number determined in Step 2.

4. Add 3 to the approximate square root.

The SMOG index, which can be applied in a few minutes, provides the grade level that a student must have reached to read the text with good comprehension.

A major shortcoming of readability formulas is that they yield a grade level measure of readability. For example, a readability formula may indicate that the materials are suitable for sixth graders. Sixth grade classes vary considerably in reading ability, however, and if your sixth grade class is not "average," the formula may give a misleading assessment of the material's readability.

Several aids to facilitate use of readability formulas are available. Some of the formulas have been computerized. By simply keypunching samples of text into the computer, it will almost immediately compute and print out the grade level equivalent using one or more readability formulas. There are also consulting services and publications that provide readability grade equivalents for commonly used school texts (7).

INTERACTION OF STUDENTS WITH THE TEXT

The two procedures that are included under this heading do not use grade level norms, but provide an individualized assessment of readability involving a specific text and a specific student group. One of them is the Cloze procedure (8). The basic steps of this procedure are as follows:

1. Select several representative passages of approximately 100 words each from the text under consideration.

2. Delete every fifth word from each passage. Reproduce the passages with a blank to fill the place of each deleted word.

3. Ask students to fill in each blank with that they think is the missing word.

The Cloze procedure is based on the principle that reading comprehension involves using contextual clues in text to derive meaning. If students can use contextual clues to guess correctly sixty percent or more of the deleted words, they should be able to read the text easily. If students can guess only forty percent or less of the missing words, they will be frustrated in reading the text. Under these conditions, the text most probably is not a suitable selection.

One disadvantage of the Cloze procedure is that, unlike the inspection procedures described above, it is relatively time-consuming to administer. However, the Cloze procedure does have the major advantage of yielding an objective, individualized measure of readability.

Another procedure for assessing readability is to have a group of students read passages from the text and ask them how easy or difficult it was to read the passages. You might ask a series of questions to test their understanding of what they have read. The Group Informal Inventory provides a set of specific questions and other activities to guide use of this procedure (9).

The Annehurst Curriculum Classification System

The Annehurst Curriculum Classification System (ACCS) is a new development in curriculum materials analysis (10). ACCS uses ten characteristics — experience, intelligence, motivation, creativity, emotion-personality, sociability, verbal expression, auditory perception, and motor perception — to describe both learners and materials. Thus, it is possible to match a learner high or low in a particular characteristic with a set of materials high or low in the same characteristic. Several rules have been developed for making appropriate matches:

1. Students low in motivation, creativity, sociability, and emotion-personality need curriculum materials that are high in these characteristics in order to maximize the possibility of learner growth.

2. Students low in experience and intelligence need curriculum materials that are low in these characteristics in order to avoid frustration and the loss of interest that can come from using materials that are above them.

3. Students low in verbal expression or in any of the perceptions need materials that are appropriate in these characteristics in order to help correct difficulties with perceptual discriminations, coordination, and categorizations. Excessive use of such materials is not suggested, as this could result in discouragement and despair.

4. Advanced or "high" students may benefit from low or inappropriate materials, but will obviously develop faster with the use of curriculum materials that are rated as high. Materials classified as being low in experience and intelligence will possibly lead to frustration and boredom if they are used continually by these students. (11)

While some research findings indicate that use of the ACCS facilitates student learning (12), other findings are not so positive (13). At this time ACCS should be viewed as a promising but unproven method for guiding the curriculum materials selection process.

Learner characteristics are one of the dimensions in the *Inventory of Dimensions for Analyzing Curriculum Materials* presented in Chapter 4 (see dimension 32 in Table 3). If learner characteristics are of particular interest to you, ACCS should be considered as an aid in your analysis of curriculum materials.

CHAPTER 5 Notes

1. Roger E. Johnson and Eileen B. Vardian, "Reading, Readability and Social Studies," *The Reading Teacher* 26 (1973):483–488.

2. John Gilloland, *Readability* (London: Hodder and Stoughton, 1972); Thomas H. Estes and Joseph L. Vaughan, Jr., *Reading and Learning in the Content Classroom,* Chapter 2 (Boston: Allyn and Bacon, 1978).

3. Rudolph Flesch, "A New Readability Yardstick," *Journal of Applied Psychology* 32 (1948):221–233.

4. Edgar Dale and Jeanne S. Chall, "A Formula for Predicting Readability," *Educational Research Bulletin* 27 (1948): 11–20, 37–54.

5. H. McLaughlin, "Smog Grading — A New Readability Formula," *Journal of Reading* 22 (1969):639–646.

6. E. A. Fry, "A Readability Formula That Saves Time," *Journal of Reading* 7 (1968):513–516.

7. Gwyneth Britton, *A Consumer's Guide to Sex, Race, and Career Bias in Public School Textbooks* (Corvallis, Oregon: Britton and Associates, 1977).

8. John R. Bormouth, "Readability: A New Approach," *Reading Research Quarterly* 1 (1966):79–132.

9. Ernest K. Dishner and John E. Readence, "Getting Started: Using the Textbook Diagnostically," *Reading World* 17 (1977):36–49.

10. Jack R. Frymier, *The Annehurst Curriculum Classification System: A Practical Way to Individualize Instruction* (West Lafayette, Ind.: Kappa Delta Pi, 1977).

11. John Langrehr, "Match the Materials and the Learners," *Audiovisual Instruction* 23 (1978):19–22.

12. Catherine Cornbleth, "Curriculum Materials and Pupil Involvement in Learning Activity," paper presented at the annual meeting of the American Educational Research Association, San Francisco, April 1979.

13. Louis P. Berneman and Carroll V. Dexter, "Annehurst Curriculum Classification System: Effects of Matching Materials and Students on Achievement, on Task Behavior, and Interest," paper presented at the annual meeting of the American Educational Research Association, San Francisco, April 1979.

CHAPTER 5 Bibliography

Reeder, Alan F., and Bolen, Jacqueline M. "Match the Materials to the Learner." *Audiovisual Instruction* 21 (1976):24–25.

6 *Appraisal of Curriculum Materials*

Teachers are sometimes disappointed when it comes time to use materials they or others have selected. The materials may be over the students' heads, or may not correspond well to the teacher's instructional goals. These problems and others can be avoided if materials are properly evaluated before making an adoption decision. In this chapter I present three strategies for evaluating the quality of curriculum materials: making a personal inspection of the materials, reading critical reviews or technical reports, and field testing. Also included is a list of 39 evaluative criteria that can be used in judging a set of curriculum materials.

Chapters 4 and 5 stressed the importance of carefully analyzing and describing the curriculum materials being considered for adoption. Without this step, you cannot do a defensible appraisal of the materials. For example, one of your criteria for evaluating materials may be their expense; Are they affordable given your needs and budget? You cannot answer this question well unless you have accurate cost data (see dimension 2 in Chapter 4).

Assuming that you have carefully analyzed and described an array of curriculum materials, the next step is to appraise their quality and effectiveness, through three strategies. The first involves a set of techniques for *inspecting the materials themselves* to determine their worth. The second strategy is to *read critical reviews or technical reports* of evaluation studies done by the developers or evaluators. The third strategy is to *conduct a field test of the materials.*

Under ideal conditions one might want to use all three of the evaluation strategies before making an adoption decision. In the real world of educational practice, though, you may be limited to just one of the strategies. The advantages of each strategy are discussed here so you can choose the one(s) most suited to your needs and resources.

STRATEGY ONE
Inspection of Curriculum Materials

An Inventory of Evaluation Criteria

The 39 dimensions for *analyzing* curriculum materials (see Table 1) can be transformed easily into criteria for *appraising* materials. For example, consider dimension 26, "assessment devices." If incorporation of assessment devices in the curriculum materials is important to a teacher, she or he will rate materials having such devices higher than those lacking them.

Some of the dimensions require little or no transformation to become an evaluation criterion. For example, aesthetic appeal (dimension 11) and quality of the physical materials (dimension 16) are explicitly evaluative.

Your judgment will most generally be a composite rating based on

TABLE 3   Inventory of Evaluative Criteria Stated As Adjectives

Publication and Cost

Analytic Dimension	*Bipolar Adjectives*
1. Authors	Expert . . . Unqualified
2. Cost	Expensive . . . Cheap
3. Development History	Well funded . . . Poorly funded
4. Edition	Current . . . Earlier (in the sense of, "an earlier edition")
5. Publication Date	Recent . . . Old
6. Publisher	Reputable . . . Unreliable
7. Purchase Procedures	Easy . . . Difficult
8. Quantity	Sufficient . . . Insufficient
9. Special Requirements	Easy (to satisfy) . . . Cumbersome (difficult to satisfy)
10. Teacher Training	Simple . . . Complex

Physical Properties

Analytic Dimension	*Bipolar Adjectives*
11. Aesthetic Appeal	Beautiful . . . Ugly
12. Components	Few . . . Many
13. Consumables	Few . . . Many
14. Durability	Sturdy . . . Flimsy
15. Media	Appropriate . . . Inappropriate
16. Quality	Fine . . . Poor
17. Safety	Safe . . . Dangerous

Content

Analytic Dimension	*Bipolar Adjectives*
18. Approach	Sound . . . Weak
19. Instructional Objectives	Clear . . . Unclear
20. Instructional Objectives — Types	Classified clearly . . . Classified unclearly
21. Issues Orientation	Sensitive to alternative views . . . Onesided
22. Multiculturalism	Multicultural . . . Ethnocentric
23. Scope and Sequence	Appropriate . . . Overly broad/narrow
24. Sex Roles	Unstereotyped . . . Stereotyped
25. Time-boundedness	Current . . . Dated

Instructional Properties

Analytic Dimension	*Bipolar Adjectives*
26. Assessment Devices	Helpful . . . Not helpful
27. Comprehensibility	Clear . . . Unclear

28.	Coordination with the Curriculum	Compatible (with other materials) . . . Incompatible
29.	Individualization	Individualized . . . Non-individualized
30.	Instructional Effectiveness	Known (to be effective) . . . Unknown
31.	Instructional Patterns	Interesting . . . Boring
32.	Learner Characteristics	Appropriate . . . Inappropriate
33.	Length	Flexible . . . Rigid
34.	Management System	Helpful . . . Not helpful
35.	Motivational Properties	Exciting . . . Dull
36.	Prerequisites	Clear . . . Unclear
37.	Readability	Comprehensible . . . Incomprehensible
38.	Role of Student	Active . . . Passive
39.	Role of Teacher	Active . . . Passive

several criteria, rather than a single criterion. The criteria can be established during the inspection of materials, but this relies too heavily on the rater's, casual, off-the-cuff decisions, and important criteria might be overlooked. To avoid this problem, it is best to formulate the criteria systematically prior to the inspection process.

An awareness of the range of available criteria can help you formulate your own. While the inventory can be stated in a variety of formats the most common involve the statement of criteria as adjectives or questions. Some adjectives that can be used to rate curriculum materials are: inexpensive, motivating, readable, durable, individualized. Table 3 presents a sample inventory of adjectives that correspond to the 39 analytic dimensions presented in Chapter 4, with the positive and negative ends of each dimension represented by bipolar adjectives, e.g., safe-dangerous.

Most of the adjectives do not constitute "either/or" criteria, that is, either the product meets the criterion or it doesn't. Instead, most adjectives represent a continuum, such that the quality represented by each adjective has several distinguishable values. For example, consider the criterion of durability. A set of materials could be rated as "durable" or "not durable," but it may be more meaningful to form a continuum, such as:

Durable (Sturdy)			**Not Durable (Flimsy)**	
5	4	3	2	1

In this example, each product is rated for durability on a five-point scale. (You may prefer to have more or fewer points on your own scales.)

The other commonly used format for stating evaluation criteria is to express them as questions. To illustrate, we can refer to the preceding paragraph in which the criterion of durability was rated on a five-point adjective scale. The same criterion could be rated by asking the question, "How durable are these materials likely to be?"

An advantage in using questions is that they can be stated precisely to meet a specific need and context. An example is this question: "Are these materials likely to last for five years if they are used daily in our district's eighth grade classes in social studies?" Persons inspecting the materials to answer this question could give a simple "yes or no" answer or a more elaborated response.

Appendix D presents an inventory of evaluation-related questions corresponding to the 39 analytic dimensions. The inventory is not exhaustive. Additional questions can be generated for each dimension, and each question can be restated to make it either more general or more specific.

Published General Checklists

Before developing your own evaluation checklist, you may wish to consider whether an already developed checklist meets your needs. Checklists for evaluating curriculum materials appear occasionally in educational journals and in books on curriculum and instruction. Some of these, such as the checklists shown below, are general and therefore can be adapted to evaluate most kinds of curriculum materials:

Abt, Clark C. "How to Compare Curriculum Materials." *Nation's Schools* 86 (1970):21–28. The author presents a comprehensive checklist for evaluating curriculum materials. The checklist includes 34 criteria organized into three categories: coverage; appropriateness; and motivational effectiveness. There also are procedures for differential weighting of criteria and for computing qualitative effectiveness and cost effectiveness.

Bleil, Gordon. "Evaluating Educational Materials." *Journal of Learning Disabilities* 8 (1975):19–26. The author includes a few recommendations specifically intended for special educators, but most of his evaluation guidelines are general in nature. The author's list of 41 questions to use in evaluating curriculum materials is organized under these headings: teacher needs; student needs; and general needs.

Fetter, Wayne R. "An Evaluation Instrument for Instructional Materials." *Educational Technology* (1978):55–56. The author presents a comprehensive instrument for describing and evaluating curriculum materials. The instrument contains a checklist of 25 items organized under the headings of appropriateness, content, organization, quality of the technical or teacher's manual, and evaluation procedures.

Tyler, Louise L.; Klein, M. Frances; and associates. *Evaluating and Choosing Curriculum and Instructional Materials.* Educational Resources Associates, 1100 Glendon Ave., Suite 900, Los Angeles, CA., 90024. The authors present a detailed set of evaluation criteria and several studies of their application to the appraisal of curriculum materials. Two checklists for evaluating materials are presented on pages 175–178.

Published Specialized Checklists

Some evaluation checklists have been developed and published for specialized use. The following is an example of this type of checklist:

Parsons, Jerry and others. "Criteria for Selecting, Evaluating or Developing Learning Modules." *Educational Technology* (1976):31–32. The authors provide procedures for the evaluation of learning modules, which are self-contained packages dealing with one specific subject matter unit and intended specifically for individualized instruction. The authors' criteria consist of 31 questions organized into seven areas: objectives; subject matter; design characteristics; learning activities; adaptability; validity; and evaluation.

You might search for other published checklists to meet your specialized needs by consulting curriculum specialists, reference works, and indexes to education literature such as *Research in Education* and *Current Index to Journals in Education* (1).

Published Checklists to Detect Sex and Ethnic Bias

Educators are becoming increasingly sensitive to the fact that some curriculum materials contain biased content. A recent study (2) has documented ethnic bias and other distortions present in American history textbooks over the past century. Educators are concerned, too, about sex bias, as exemplified by this statement in a career education product allegedly free of sex bias, "If you're a girl, you'd probably rather handle curlers than tools" (3). Sex role stereotyping has been found in preschool picture books (4), basal readers (5), social studies texts (6), math texts (7), and even in textbooks for teacher education (8)!

Stereotyping is just one type of sex and ethnic bias. Six different types of bias that can be found in curriculum materials are listed in Table 4 (9).

TABLE 4   Types of Sex and Ethnic Bias

1. *Invisibility:* Certain groups are underrepresented in curricular materials. The significant omission of women and minority groups has become so great as to imply that these groups are of less value, importance, and significance in our society.

2. *Stereotyping:* By assigning traditional and rigid roles or attributes to a group, instructional materials stereotype and limit the abilities and potential of that group. Not only are careers stereotyped, but so, too, are intellectual abilities, personality characteristics, physical appearance, social status and domestic roles. Stereotyping denies students a knowledge of the diversity, complexity and variation of any group of individuals. Children who see themselves portrayed only in stereotypic ways may internalize those stereotypes and fail to develop their own unique abilities, interests and full potential.

3. *Imbalance/Selectivity:* Textbooks perpetuate bias by presenting only one interpretation of an issue, situation, or group of people. This imbalanced account restricts the knowledge of students regarding the varied perspectives which may apply to a particular situation. Through selective presentation of materials, textbooks distort reality and ignore complex and differing viewpoints. As a result, millions of students have been taught little or nothing about the contributions, struggles, and participation of women and minorities in our society.

4. *Unreality:* Textbooks frequently present an unrealistic portrayal of our history and our contemporary life experience. Controversial topics are glossed over and discussions of discrimination and prejudice are avoided. This unrealistic coverage denies children the information they need to recognize, understand, and perhaps some day conquer the problems that plague our society.

5. *Fragmentation/Isolation:* By separating issues related to minorities and women from the main body of the text, instructional materials imply that these issues are less important than and not a part of the dominant culture. The practice of isolating female and minority issues teaches students that these issues are only a diversion, unrelated to the main theme and events of the text.

6. *Linguistic Bias:* Curricular materials reflect the discriminatory nature of our language. Masculine terms and pronouns, ranging from our "forefathers" to the generic "he," deny the participation of women in our society. Further, occupations, such as "mailman" are given masculine labels that deny the legitimacy of women working in these fields. Imbalance of word order* and lack of parallel terms that refer to females and males are also forms of linguistic bias.

Source: Shirley McCune and Martha Matthews, ed. *Implementing Title IX and Attaining Sex Equity: A Workshop Package for Postsecondary Educators* (Washington, D.C.: U.S. Government Printing Office, 1978).
* e.g., always using the phrase, "he and she," rather than varying it by saying "she and he."

The following are several examples of published checklists and procedures for detecting sex and ethnic bias in curriculum materials:

Banks, James A. "Evaluating and Selecting Ethnic Studies Materials." *Educational Leadership* 31 (1974):593–596. This journal article presents criteria for evaluating ethnic studies resources.

Britton & Associates, Inc. Instructional Materials Analysis Services. 1054 NW Fillmore, Corvallis, OR 97330. This service provides objective analyses of curriculum materials to determine the extent to which they contain sex, race, and career bias. The procedures used by this service are presented in several publications (available from the above address): *Revised Textbook Analysis Kit for Careers, Sex, Race; Consumers Guide to Sex, Race, & Career Bias in Public School Textbooks*.

Dunfee, Maxine, ed. *Eliminating Ethnic Bias in Instructional Materials: Comment and Bibliography*. Washington, D.C.: Association for Supervision and Curriculum Development, 1974. This publication contains a twenty-item checklist that assesses various aspects of sex and ethnic bias.

Pratt, David. *How to Find and Measure Bias in Textbooks*. Englewood Cliffs, N.J.: Educational Technology Publications, 1972. This brief pamphlet describes an objective procedure for detecting the presence of ethnic bias in curriculum materials. The procedure is based on a count of favorable and unfavorable terms used to refer to a particular minority group.

Detection of Advertising Bias

As noted in Chapter 4, many of the free curriculum materials available to teachers are published and distributed by business and industry. These materials need to be examined carefully to determine whether they reflect the biases of the particular industry distributing them. Also, the materials should be reviewed to determine whether they are advertising, either explicitly or incidentally, a particular commercial product. Although I am not aware of published checklists for this purpose, these criteria appear relevant: Is the content of the industry-sponsored materials accurate or false? Is it likely to be misleading? Is it likely to be deceptive?

Sheila Harty has conducted an extensive survey of industry-sponsored materials (9). The following is one example of the bias she found in some of these materials:

The *American Tobacco Story* is a glossy, full-color, illustrated booklet available to teachers upon request from the American Tobacco Company, division of American Brands, Inc. The booklet opens with the amazing credit:

> *Cigarettes and civilization — the two seem to go together.* (page 3)

Further on we read:

> *Many of the common sailors were quick to learn that tobacco satisfies a human need.* (page 7)

The industry trade association, the Tobacco Institute, responds to requests from teachers for materials with full classroom sets of eight pamphlets and eleven booklets illustrating tobacco production in selected states; posters and other color-illustrated booklets are also available. These materials focus on the historical and economic value of tobacco. Nowhere on the materials, nor on the illustrations of cigarette packages, does the Surgeon General's warning appear. Nicotine and its addictive characteristics are not mentioned, nor are other health hazards from smoking. The only laboratory research on smoking mentioned was that motivated to improve its taste. These are omissions so significant as to render the materials deceptive and misleading. (10)

Criteria for Instructional Effectiveness

In evaluating curriculum materials, we can easily become preoccupied with criteria such as cost, durability, aesthetic appeal, and content coverage. We may forget that the real purpose of curriculum materials is to help students learn. The materials can cover the right content, be durable, etc., and yet be a poor instructional tool.

What features make some curriculum materials an effective instructional tool and others a hindrance to learning? Research findings are not definitive, but they do suggest a variety of features that can be incorporated in curriculum materials to enhance their effectiveness (11). A list of these features, each of which has been supported directly or indirectly by research, is presented in Appendix E.

The features can be used as criteria for evaluating curriculum materials. Materials that contain many of the features are likely to be more effective — in the sense of facilitating the learning process — than materials that contain a few or none of them. In the absence of field-test data, the reviewer may need to rely on an inspection of these features to make a judgment about the materials' effectiveness.

Sigmund Tobias has done research (12) that relates to the features of materials presented in Appendix E. He found that the "instructional support" provided by curriculum materials (defined in terms of some of the features presented in Appendix E) is more important for low aptitude students than for high aptitude students, and more important for students who are just beginning a new subject than for students who already have learned a fair amount about the subject. These findings appeal to our common sense; it seems reasonable that very bright or advanced students could manage to learn from poorly constructed curriculum materials, but that low-achieving or beginning students would likely be hindered by such materials.

The lesson to be learned from Tobias's research is that it is important to check materials for the presence of the "instructional support" features described in Appendix E when the intended audience is low-achieving or beginning students.

STRATEGY TWO
Inspection of Evaluative Data

Published Reviews

Critical reviews of curriculum materials appear as a regular feature of many education journals, such as *The Mathematics Teacher, Instructor, Audiovisual Instruction*, and *Appraisal*. In addition, there are education journals that are devoted primarily to reviews. Educators are likely to find the following journals most relevant to their needs:

1. *Booklist*, published twice monthly, September through July, and once in August. Reviews books, films, filmstrips, and sound recordings for all grade levels.

2. *Curriculum Review*, published five times annually. Reviews textbooks and supplementary materials in all areas of the K-12 curriculum. Language arts, mathematics, science, and social studies are usually covered in each issue.

3. *Previews*, published monthly, September through May. Reviews videocasettes, 16mm films, filmstrips, slides, kits, and sound recordings.

4. *School Library Journal*, published monthly, September through May. Reviews books written for K-12 students.

If you wish to know whether there are published reviews of a particular curriculum product, *Media Review Digest* (MRD) is available as an index to reviews, evaluations, and descriptions of all forms of non-book media for all grade levels. The MRD is published annually, with a semiannual supplement. A useful feature of the MRD is that it provides a brief digest of the reviews available for each curriculum product.

If you are interested in identifying reviews of books, the *Current Book Review Citations* (CBRC) is a useful resource. CBRC is an author and title index to book reviews published in more than twelve hundred periodicals. The reviews cover general fiction and non-fiction, as well as books for children and young adults. Other indexes to book reviews are *Book Review Digest* and *Book Review Index.*

Reviews should be read with a critical eye. The situation is somewhat like reading movie reviews. You probably have had the experience of reading two reviews of the same movie — one positive and one negative. Your own impression of the movie, after actually seeing it, might not agree with any of the published reviews.

The process of reading a review *critically* can be accomplished by asking yourself four questions. First, is the reviewer qualified to evaluate the materials? Second, is the review based on one reviewer's judgment or on the judgment of several (e.g., a review panel)? Third, does the reviewer have clear criteria for evaluating the materials? And fourth, does the reviewer substantiate his or her judgment with specific, objective data? Although the first two questions are difficult to answer, since reviewers' names and qualifications sometimes are not stated, the third and fourth questions can be answered by careful reading of the review.

Even under the best of conditions, you probably should not make a selection decision solely on the basis of a published review. If the review is favorable, you should take the next step of inspecting the materials yourself. If the review is negative, you may wish to inspect the materials, especially if no alternative materials are available.

Technical Reports

A very small percentage of curriculum materials have been validated through field-testing. The situation is improving, however, especially for federally sponsored curriculum projects. These projects must include an evaluation component to qualify for funding.

The results of an evaluation study sometimes are summarized in a technical report. A well-designed evaluation study typically includes students who use the curriculum materials (the "experimental group") and students who either do not use the materials or who use a competing product (the "control" group). The study's purpose is to determine whether the experimental group of students outperforms the control group. Performance is assessed by administering cognitive, affective, or psychomotor measures, which may be in the form of written tests or observations of students' behavior. Most evaluation studies focus on short-term direct effects of curriculum materials. More sophisticated studies may examine long-term and transfer effects.

As with published reviews of curriculum materials, technical reports should be read critically. The conclusions of evaluation studies may reflect *measurement deficiencies and errors of research design* rather than *real effects* of curriculum materials. For example, a test used to measure learning gains may be invalid or low in reliability. A test having these deficiencies would be insensitive to real effects of the materials. A relatively common problem of research design occurs when teachers in the field test use curriculum materials under ideal conditions not usually found in schools. If this situation occurs, learning gains found in the field test provide a poor guarantee for the purchaser who intends to use them under different conditions.

The critical reader of technical reports also should determine whether the evaluator measured some effects of the materials, but failed to measure other effects. It is possible that the materials have negative side effects that went unrecorded by the evaluators. For example, the materials may increase students' knowledge about the curriculum content (a measured effect), but also may cause students to develop a biased attitude toward the content (an unmeasured effect).

The results of evaluation studies usually are reported in terms of group trends. A statistical average such as the mean or median is used to summarize the performance of an entire group of students. When this occurs, the critical reader should ask whether it is likely that the curriculum materials have the same effect on all students; for example, materials may be effective for high aptitude students but not for low aptitude students.

Technical reports usually are prepared during the period that the materials are being developed. They rarely are distributed by the publisher as part of the completed curriculum product. Therefore, it is usually necessary to contact the original developers to determine whether evaluation studies were conducted and whether they are presented in an accessible technical report.

Publishers' Promotional Material

Like any other advertising, publishers' promotional devices serve a useful purpose: they inform educators of new material that can meet instructional needs. On the other hand, publishers' advertising sometimes "create" superficial needs. Advertisements may make unwarranted or inaccurate claims about the materials' content and effectiveness. One typical claim is that the materials are "high interest" or "easy to learn from."

As with evaluative reviews, publishers' promotional materials should be read critically, and a selection decision should not be based solely on publishers' claims. Such claims should be substantiated by applying other evaluation strategies, by making a personal inspection of the materials, by reading evaluative reviews, or by field-testing the materials.

Word-of-Mouth

Educators frequently learn about new educational materials and programs by talking with colleagues. This strategy has several advantages. Talking with fellow educators is often more enjoyable than poring over catalogs of materials, and, if you know the educator personally, you have a basis for judging his or her credibility. (A problem with reading published reviews, as I noted earlier, is that the reviewer's name and qualifications sometimes are not provided.) Another advantage of word-of-mouth is that if the educator has used the materials, you can benefit from his or her experiences.

Word-of-mouth promotion also has drawbacks. One's colleagues like reviewers or publishers, may be biased. Also, an educator may not want to admit that his or her school district made a mistake in purchasing a particular set of materials, especially if they are expensive. In this situation the educator might deny or downplay the materials' faults in order to avoid embarrassment.

In summary, word-of-mouth can provide useful evaluative data about curriculum materials under certain conditions. It is doubtful whether one should ever rely exclusively on this data source, however. If a colleague recommends a particular curriculum product, one should supplement the recommendation with at least one of the other evaluation strategies described in this chapter.

STRATEGY THREE
Field Testing the Curriculum Materials

Purpose of a Field Test

How often have you had the experience of purchasing a product, bringing it home, and then finding that it did not perform as you imagined or as advertisements claimed it would? Curriculum products are subject to the same problem. Most educators are concerned — with good justification — that materials developed elsewhere will not work in their local situation. Even if field test data are available in a technical report, one can legitimately ask whether the data apply to a different school context.

If you have reason to believe that this is a problem, you should consider doing a local field test, the purpose of which is to determine the effectiveness of materials in a specific instructional context. The term "field test" connotes a fairly substantial amount of experimentation, although this need not be the case. You may be more comfortable with the term "pilot test" or "feasibility test" if your test of the materials is modest in scope.

Because even a small field test requires time and other resources, you should consider whether such a test is necessary before making an adoption decision. The following are examples of situations in which a field test appears warranted:

- when the materials are quite different in instructional format or content than those generally used.

- when inspection of the materials (see Evaluation Strategy One) does not provide a clear indication of how they would work in the classroom.

- when reliable data on the materials' effectiveness are not available elsewhere.

- when the materials are expensive.

- when the materials will play an important role in the curriculum. A field test probably is most justified when one or both of the last two conditions are present.

Field Test Procedures

As stated above, field tests are most needed when the curriculum materials under consideration are expensive and are to play a central role in the curriculum. After determining that a field test is necessary, it should be planned carefully to insure useful evaluation data. There is no point in designing a field test that yields more data than one actually needs. First, consider the number of teachers and students to be included in the sample. A few teachers and their classes should be sufficient to obtain a clear indication of the strengths and weaknesses of a curriculum product. Unless one has ample resources, it is difficult to track the progress of a large number of teachers as they use the product. Also, there is no point in frustrating a large sample of teachers if the product proves to be ineffective. They can learn vicariously from the few teachers included in the field test sample.

The second consideration in designing a field test is how much of the curriculum package to field test. Since curriculum materials usually have repetitive instructional patterns (see Chapter 5), it may be possible to limit the number of instructional units included in the field test. Even a few days of instruction with a set of curriculum materials may give the teacher a clear indication of the materials' strengths and weaknesses.

The third consideration involves deciding how closely the field test will parallel actual classroom teaching conditions. It is possible to imagine a simulated field test in which teachers try out the materials in a workshop setting. Some of the teachers can play the role of instructors and others can play the role of students. Another possibility is to ask selected students to study the materials outside the regular classroom situation; this might be done as an extra credit assignment. In most instances, though, it probably is advisable to conduct the field test under conditions that closely approximate those for which the materials were designed.

The fourth, important consideration in planning a field test is to carefully identify the types of data to be collected and the procedures for collecting them. A sophisticated field test might involve a collection of student performance on tests developed specifically to measure the materials' instructional objectives. Also, one might design an instrument for recording data based on personal observations of the materials in use. Most field tests, however, are less ambitious. They rely on questionnaires administered after the materials have been in use for some time.

An alternative to the questionnaire is the interview. The advantage of interviews is that they generally yield a "richer" base of evaluative data. This advantage occurs because some people express themselves more openly in an interview situation than with questionnaires or tests and because the interviewer can probe the person's responses. Since the individual interview is time-consuming, one might consider administering an interview only to a few teachers and students in the sample. A parallel questionnaire can be administered to the other field test participants.

Learner Verification and Revision

Field-testing of curriculum materials prior to publication has two important benefits. First, field test results can help potential purchasers predict how well the materials may work in practice. And second, field-testing may suggest how the materials can be improved prior to publication.

Some educators have been sufficiently impressed with these benefits that they advocate field-testing of all curriculum materials prior to general distribution. Kenneth Komoski, president of Educational Products Information Exchange (EPIE), has been a particularly strong advocate of field-testing, which he labels *learner verification and revision* (LVR). The process of LVR involves determining the effectiveness of a set of curriculum materials by using them with a sample of the students for whom they are intended. If weaknesses in the materials are revealed through the verification process, the publishers should make appropriate revisions. In fact, there is research evidence that LVR results in more effective curriculum materials

(13). Unfortunately, it is estimated that less than one percent of all curriculum materials in use in the United States have incorporated any form of LVR (14).

Guidelines for implementing the LVR process have been suggested by Kenneth Komoski and others (15). For example, the process of LVR should begin while the materials are under development and should continue for as long as they are on the market. Also, LVR data should come directly from learners; teachers, parents, and others should be considered only as supplemental sources of data. Another guideline is that LVR data should be sufficiently detailed to enable the developer and purchaser to identify clearly the materials' strong and weak points.

Although the concept of LVR is relatively new, it already has influenced statewide adoption of new curriculum materials. For example, California and Florida have passed legislation that requires publishers to include LVR evidence with curriculum products that they wish to submit for state adoption or recommendation. The following is quoted from Florida Senate Bill 492, section 283.25:

> Publishers shall provide written proof of the use of the learner verification and revision process during prepublication development and post-publication revision of the materials in question. For purpose of this section learner verification is defined as the empirical process of data gathering and analysis by which a publisher of a curriculum material has improved the instructional effectiveness of that product before it reaches the market and then continues to gather data from learners in order to improve the quality and reliability of that material during its full market life.

LVR legislation is now pending in seventeen other states.

Several controversies and problems in implementing the LVR process have been identified (16). They are worth overcoming, however, because of LVR's potential for facilitating the development of worthwhile and effective curriculum materials.

CHAPTER 6 Notes

1. These are publications of the Educational Resources Information Clearinghouse (ERIC). ERIC publications are available in many school districts and in most universities and colleges.

2. Frances FitzGerald, *America Revised* (Boston: Little, Brown, 1979).

3. *Phi Delta Kappan* 57 (1976):427.

4. Lenore J. Weitzman, Deborah Eifler, Elizabeth Hokada, and Catherine Ross, "Sex-role Socialization in Picture Books for Preschool Children," *American Journal of Sociology* 77 (1972):1125–1150.

5. Women on Words and Images, *Dick and Jane as Victims: Sex Stereotyping in Children's Readers* (Princeton, N.J.: Women on Words and Images, 1975).

6. Karen DeCrow, "Look, Jane, Look! See Dick Run and Jump! Admire Him!" In *Sex Differences and Discrimination in Education,* ed. S. Anderson (Worthington, Ohio: Charles A. Jones, 1972).

7. B. Levy and J. Stacey, "Sexism in the Elementary School: A Backward and Forward Look," *Phi Delta Kappan* 55 (1973):105–109.

8. Myra Sadker and David Sadker, *Beyond Pictures and Pronouns: Sexism in Teacher Education Textbooks* (Washington, D.C.: The American University, n.d.) .

9. Sheila Harty, *Hucksters in the Classroom: A Review of Industry Propaganda in Schools* (Washington, D.C.: Center for Study of Responsive Law, 1979).

10. Ibid., page 121.

11. Research relevant to the list in Appendix E is reviewed in these sources: Harold W. Faw and T. Gary Waller, "Mathemagenic Behaviors and Efficiency in Learning from Prose Materials," *Review of Educational Research* 46 (1976): 691–720; Robert M. Gagné and Leslie J. Briggs, *Principles of Instructional Design,* 2nd ed. (New York: Holt, Rinehart and Winston, 1979); James Hartley and Ivor K. Davies, "Preinstructional Strategies: The Role of Pretests, Behavioral Objectives, Overviews and Advance Organizers," *Review of Educational Research* 46 (1976):239–265.

12. Sigmund Tobias, "Achievement Treatment Interactions," *Review of Educational Research* 46 (1976):61–74.

13. The research evidence is reviewed in: Harold D. Stolovitch, "The Intermediate Technology of Learner Verification and Revision (LVR)," *Educational Technology* 18 (1978):13–17.

14. P. Kenneth Komoski, "An Imbalance of Product Quantity and Instructional Quality: The Imperative of Empiricism," *AV Communication Review* 22 (1974).

15. P. Kenneth Komoski, "Learner Verification: Touchstone for Instructional Materials?" *Educational Leadership* 31 (1974):397–399.

16. M. Francis Klein, *About Learning Materials* (Washington, D.C.: Association for Supervision and Curriculum Development, 1978):19–23.

CHAPTER 6 Bibliography

Eash, Maurice J. "Developing an Instrument for Assessing Instructional Materials. In *Evaluating Educational Performance: A Sourcebook of Methods, Instruments, and Examples.* Edited by Herbert J. Walberg. Berkeley, Calif.: McCutchan, 1974.

"Evaluation and Selection of Media: Theme Issue." *Audiovisual Instruction* 20: (April 1975):1–74.

Hodgson, Beverly J. "Sex, Texts, and the First Amendment." *Journal of Law-Education* 5 (1976):173–195.

McLaughlin, John A., and Trlica, Jack S. "Teacher Evaluation of Instructional Materials." *Educational Technology* 16 (1976):51–54.

Niedermeyer, Fred C., and Moncrief, Michael H. "Guidelines for Selecting Effective Instructional Products." *Elementary School Journal* 76 (1975):127–131.

Weston, Louise C., and Stein, Sandra L. "A Content Analysis of Publishers' Guidelines for the Elimination of Sex-role Stereotyping." *Educational Researcher* 7 (1978):13–14.

Appendix A
Guidelines for Interpreting the "Fair Use" Provisions of the New Copyright Laws

*This appendix contains specific guidelines for inter-
preting the "fair use" provisions (Section 107) of the
new copyright laws. The first set of guidelines, which
refer to the reproduction of copyrighted printed materials, was prepared in 1976 by three organizations:
the Authors League of America; the Association of
American Publishers; and the Ad Hoc Committee of
Educational Institutions and Organizations on Copyrighted Law Revision. The second set of guidelines in
this appendix refers to the reproduction of copyrighted
musical works. They were prepared by representatives
of the Music Publishers Association of the United
States, the National Music Publishers Association, the
Music Teachers National Association, the Music Educators National Conference, the National Association
of Schools of Music, and the Ad Hoc Committee of
Educational Institutions and Organizations on Copyright Law Revision.*

I. COPYING OF PRINTED MATERIALS
Agreement on Guidelines for Classroom Copying in Not-For-Profit Educational Institutions with Respect to Books and Periodicals

The purpose of the following guidelines is to state the minimum standards of educational fair use under Section 107 of H.R. 2223. The parties agree that the conditions determining the extent of permissible copying for educational purposes may change in the future; that certain types of copying permitted under these guidelines may not be permissible in the future; and conversely that in the future other types of copying not permitted under these guidelines may be permissible under revised guidelines.

Moreover, the following statement of guidelines is not intended to limit the types of copying permitted under the standards of fair use under judicial decision and which are stated in Section 107 of the Copyright Revision Bill. There may be instances in which copying which does not fall within the guidelines stated below may nonetheless be permitted under the criteria of fair use.

Guidelines

I. *Single Copying for Teachers*

A single copy may be made of any of the following by or for a teacher at his or her individual request for his or her scholarly research or use in teaching or preparation to teach a class:

A. A chapter from a book;

B. An article from a periodical or newspaper;

C. A short story, short essay or short poem, whether or not from a collective work;

D.   A chart, graph, diagram, drawing, cartoon or picture from a book, periodical, or newspaper;

II.   *Multiple Copies for Classroom Use*

Multiple copies (not to exceed in any event more than one copy per pupil in a course) may be made by or for the teacher giving the course for classroom use or discussion; *provided that:*

A.   The copying meets the test of brevity and spontaneity as defined below; *and,*

B.   Meets the cumulative effect test as defined below; *and,*

C.   Each copy includes a notice of copyright

DEFINITIONS

Brevity
(*i*) Poetry: (a) A complete poem if less than 250 words and if printed on not more than two pages or, (b) from a longer poem, an excerpt of not more than 250 words.

(*ii*) Prose: (a) Either a complete article, story or essay of less than 2,500 words, or (b) an excerpt from any prose work of not more than 1,000 words or 10% of the work, whichever is less, but in any event a minimum of 500 words.

[Each of the numerical limits stated in "i" and "ii" above may be expanded to permit the completion of an unfinished line of a poem or of an unfinished prose paragraph.]

(*iii*) Illustration: One chart, graph, diagram, drawing, cartoon or picture per book or per periodical issue.

(*iv*) "Special" works: Certain works in poetry, prose or in "poetic prose" which often combine language with illustrations and which are intended sometimes for children and at other times for a more general audience fall short of 2,500 words in their entirety. Paragraph "ii" above notwithstanding such "special works" may not be reproduced in their entirety; however, an excerpt comprising not more than two of the published pages of such special work and containing not more than 10% of the words found in the text thereof, may be reproduced.

Spontaneity
(*i*) The copying is at the instance and inspiration of the individual teacher, and

(*ii*) The inspiration and decision to use the work and the moment of its use for maximum teaching effectiveness are so close in time that it would be unreasonable to expect a timely reply to a request for permission.

Cumulative Effect
(*i*) The copying of the material is for only one course in the school in which the copies are made.

(*ii*) Not more than one short poem, article, story, essay or two excerpts may be copied from the same author, nor more than three from the same collective work or periodical volume during one class term.

(*iii*) There shall not be more than nine instances of such multiple copying for one course during one class term.

[The limitations stated in "ii" and "iii" above shall not apply to current news periodicals and newspapers and current news sections of other periodicals.]

III.   *Prohibitions as to I and II Above*

Notwithstanding any of the above, the following shall be prohibited:

(A) Copying shall not be used to create or to replace or substitute for anthologies, compilations or collective works. Such replacement or substitution may occur whether copies of various works or excerpts therefrom are accumulated or reproduced and used separately.

(B) There shall be no copying of or from works intended to be "consumable" in the course of study or of teaching. These include workbooks, exercises, standardized tests and test booklets and answer sheets and like consumable material.

(C) Copyright shall not:
- (a) substitute for the purchase of books, publishers' reprints or periodicals;
- (b) be directed by higher authority;
- (c) be repeated with respect to the same item by the same teacher from term to term.

(D) No charge shall be made to the student beyond the actual cost of the photocopying.

Agreed March 19, 1976.

Ad Hoc Committee on Copyright Law Revision:

By Sheldon Elliott Steinbach.

Author-Publisher Group:
Authors League of America:

By Irwin Karp, *Counsel.*

Association of American Publishers, Inc.:

By Alexander C. Hoffman,
Chairman, Copyright Committee.

II. GUIDELINES FOR EDUCATIONAL USES OF MUSIC

The purpose of the following guidelines is to state the minimum and not the maximum standards of educational fair use under Section 107 of HR 2223. The parties agree that the conditions determining the extent of permissible copying for educational purposes may change in the future; that certain types of copying permitted under these guidelines may not be permissible in the future, and conversely that in the future other types of copying not permitted under these guidelines may be permissible under revised guidelines.

Moreover, the following statement of guidelines is not intended to limit the types of copying permitted under the standards of fair use under judicial decision and which are stated in Section 107 of the Copyright Revision Bill. There may be instances in which copying which does not fall within the guidelines stated below may nonetheless be permitted under the criteria of fair use.

Permissible Uses

1. Emergency copying to replace purchased copies which for any reason are not available for an imminent performance provided purchased replacement copies shall be substituted in due course.

2. (a) For academic purposes other than performance, multiple copies of excerpts of works may be made, provided that the excerpts do not comprise a part of the whole which would constitute a performable unit such as a section, movement or aria, but in no case more than 10% of the whole work. The number of copies shall not exceed one copy per pupil.

   (b) For academic purposes other than performance, a single copy of an entire performable unit (section, movement, aria, etc.) that is, (1) confirmed by the copyright proprietor to be out of print or (2) unavailable except in a larger work, may be made by or for a teacher solely for the purpose of his or her scholarly research or in preparation to teach a class.

3. Printed copies which have been purchased may be edited or simplified provided that the fundamental character of the work is not distorted or the lyrics, if any, altered or lyrics added if none exist.

4. A single copy of recordings of performances by students may be made for evaluation or rehearsal purposes and may be retained by the educational institution or individual teacher.

5. A single copy of a sound recording (such as a tape, disc or cassette) of

copyrighted music may be made from sound recordings owned by an educational institution or an individual teacher for the purpose of constructing aural exercises or examinations and may be retained by the educational institution or individual teacher. (This pertains only to the copyright of the music itself and not to any copyright which may exist in the sound recording.)

Prohibitions

1. Copying to create or replace or substitute for anthologies, compilations or collective works.

2. Copying of or from works intended to be "consumable" in the course of study or of teaching such as workbooks, exercises, standardized tests and answer sheets and like material.

3. Copying for the purpose of performance, except as in A(1) above.

4. Copying for the purpose of substituting for the purchase of music, except as in A(1) and A(2) above.

5. Copying without inclusion of the copyright notice which appears on the printed copy.

Appendix B
Example of a School District Policy
for Handling Complaints
about Curriculum Materials

From: *Media Program Guide.* Salem, Ore.: Oregon Department of Education, 1979, pages 39–43. Reprinted by permission of the Beaverton School District, Beaverton, Oregon.

Beaverton School District Board Policy

Selection of Instructional Materials

Instructional materials implement, enrich and support the educational program of the school district. To this end, a wide range of print materials with diversity of appeal, points of view and levels of reading ability will be provided.

The responsibility for the selection of instructional materials is delegated to the superintendent. The selection of instructional materials shall implement the following objectives:

1. To provide a comprehensive collection of materials which will implement, enrich, support, and extend the curriculum; and encompass the varied interests, abilities, socioeconomic backgrounds and maturity levels of the students.

2. To provide materials which will stimulate growth in the areas of factual knowledge, critical thinking, literary appreciation and aesthetic values.

3. To provide materials representative of the contributions of all people, regardless of age, sex, religion, ethnic or cultural origin.

4. To provide for coordination of instructional materials between and within elementary, intermediate and high schools.

5. To provide a background of information which will enable students to make intelligent judgments in their daily lives.

6. To provide materials on controversial issues which will enable students to develop, under guidance, critical analysis of media.

7. To place principle above personal opinion and reason above prejudice in the selection of materials of the highest quality in order to assure a comprehensive collection of materials for all students.

8. To involve teachers, administrators, students, and residents of the community in the development of criteria for the selection of materials.

Criteria developed by Beaverton School District 48 must not be in conflict with criteria approved by the State Board of Education.

9.   To provide procedures whereby residents of the community may question the use of particular instructional materials in the schools.

The superintendent is instructed to develop procedures to implement this policy.

Beaverton School District Administrative Regulations

Instructional Materials Selection

The Beaverton School District 48 Board delegates the responsibility for selecting instructional materials to the superintendent. Policy also states that teachers, administrators and residents of the community shall be involved in the process.

*Procedures for Selection of New Instructional
Materials for Multiple School Use*

The assistant superintendent for instruction shall be responsible for establishing the selection procedures, appointing appropriate committees, accepting recommendations from committees assigned to the task, and making the final decision when instructional materials for multiple school use are selected. While the specific procedure may vary depending upon the particular subject area under study, the following elements shall be present:

1.   Teachers will be involved in determining the need for adopting new instructional materials and the major areas in which the district should begin the selection process.

2.   A committee consisting of teachers, administrators, students, local school committee members, and other residents of the community, will be established to develop criteria to be used in the selection of instructional materials. The criteria developed must be consistent with existing Board policies and must not conflict with criteria developed by the State Board of Education.

3.   A committee consisting of teachers and administrators will be established to review available materials and recommend not more than five programs or sets of materials which meet the developed criteria.

4.   The assistant superintendent for instruction will review and approve programs or sets of materials submitted by the above committee and provide each school with copies of the approved materials.

5. The materials under consideration shall be available throughout the District for a period of time, not less than two weeks, for interested residents of the attendance area to review, study, and make suggestions, if they wish. Comments and recommendations from community residents will be given thorough consideration. (The instruction office will prepare standard comment sheets for use by the public.) Information concerning the availability of materials for review will be sent home in the usual written communication procedures used by individual schools. In addition, the assistant superintendent will prepare appropriate notices to be placed in local newspapers and the District 48 Report.

6. Teachers and administrators and at least one high school student, when high school materials are being considered, will choose instructional materials for use in their particular school from among the materials approved by the assistant superintendent for instruction.

Procedures for Selection of New Instructional
Materials in the Instructional Materials Center (IMC)
at the School Building Level
and the Curriculum Materials Center (CMC)
at the District Level

1. The appropriate teachers and librarian shall recommend to the principal materials to be acquired for use in the IMC. The principal or designee has the authority to approve or reject materials for use in the IMC.

2. The media specialist or appropriate personnel shall recommend to the supervisor materials to be acquired for use in and distribution through the CMC.

3. Instructional materials selected for use in an IMC or the CMC must meet the same criteria as materials selected for multiple school use.

4. The supervisor has the authority to approve or reject materials for use in the CMC.

5. In the event that material is rejected, a teacher may appeal the rejection through administrative channels.

Procedures to Request a Reconsideration
of the Use of Instructional Materials

Although care is exercised in selecting instructional materials, there will be occasions when a parent or resident may wish to request a reconsideration of the use of certain instructional materials. In such an event, the individual shall contact the teacher in an attempt to *informally* resolve the issue. If the matter cannot be resolved between the teacher and the individual calling for reconsideraion of the material, the matter will be referred to the principal. The principal shall:

1. Have the parent or resident complete the form for "Request for Reconsideration of Instructional Materials."

2. Acknowledge receipt of all written or verbal requests for reconsideration of the use of instructional materials.

3. Notify all staff members who are directly involved in the request.

4. Contact the individual who made the request to discuss the issue further and attempt to resolve it.

If the issue is not resolved in the above manner, the following formal procedures will be followed. If at any point in the procedures the issue can be resolved, the process shall be terminated.

1. The principal will forward the "Request for Reconsideration of Instructional Materials" and other appropriate correspondence to the assistant superintendent for instruction. A review committee will be established.

2. The material(s) in question shall continue to be used until the formal procedure is completed.

3. Final action on a request shall be taken by the administration no later than fifteen school days after the principal receives the completed "Request for Reconsideration of Instructional Materials."

Establishment of a Review Committee

The assistant superintendent for instruction will appoint a review committee composed of:

1. A director of elementary or secondary education (chairperson).

2. Three teachers of the same grade level or department where the material is being used.

3. One high school student.

4. The principal of the school involved.

5. Three local school committee members.

Committee Review Procedure

1. Committee members will receive copies of the statement questioning the instructional material.

2. Opportunity shall be afforded those persons or groups questioning the materials to meet with the committee and to present their opinions. The teacher and any other person involved in the selection or use of the questioned material shall also have an opportunity to meet with the committee to present their position in the matter.

3. The committee will review the material in question and form opinions based on the material taken on a whole and not on passages taken out of context.

4. The committee will formulate their recommendations and prepared written report for the assistant superintendent for instruction who will make a final determination for action.

Action Taken

1. The action taken relative to the request for reconsideration of instructional materials will be communicated in writing to the person initiating the request.

2. The final decision and supporting documentation shall be sent to all district administrators.

3. Disposition of the appeal shall be made known to all parties in the action.

In the event that issues cannot be resolved by the above process, appeals can be made directly to the superintendent.

REQUEST FOR
RECONSIDERATION OF INSTRUCTIONAL MATERIALS

Initiated by _____

           Name   Address   Telephone

Representing   Self _____ Organization or group (name) _____

Material questioned:

a. Book/Journal/Article, etc.: _____

                                   Title

_____

        Author   Publisher   Copyright Date

b. Audiovisual Material: _____

   (Film, Filmstrip, Record, etc.)   Title

c. Other Material: _____

   (Identify)

Please respond to the following questions. If more space is needed, please use an additional sheet of paper.

1. Have you seen or read this material in its entirety? _____

2. To what do you object? Please cite specific passages, pages, etc. _____

_____

_____

3. What do you believe is the main idea of this material? _____

_____

4. What do you believe might result from the use of this material? _____

_____

5. What reviews of this material have you read? _____

_____

6. For what other age group might this material be suitable? _____

_____

7. What action do you recommend that the school take on this material? _____

_____

Appendix C
Inventory of Catalogs of
Curriculum Materials

This inventory includes 96 catalogs organized under the following headings:

General Catalogs (ref. nos. 1-10)
General Catalogs: Nonprint Media (ref. nos. 11-18)
General Catalogs: Specific Age or Grade Levels (ref. nos. 19-31)
The Arts (ref. nos. 32-33)
Bilingual and Multicultural Education (ref. nos. 34-40)
Career and Consumer Education (ref. nos. 41-44)
English, Language Arts, and Reading (ref. nos. 45-49)
Foreign Languages (ref. nos. 50-52)
Mathematics and Science (ref. nos. 53-58)
Mental Health, Physical Health, Recreation, Religion, and Safety (ref. nos. 59-68)
Social Studies (ref. nos. 69-86)
Special Education (ref. nos. 87-90)
Vocational and Technical Education (ref. nos. 91-96)

The title of each catalog is followed by: cost; intended audience; number of materials described in the catalog; publication date; other descriptive data, if appropriate; and address from which the catalog can be ordered. Some catalogs are available from ERIC (Educational Resources Information Center). Further information on ERIC and this inventory can be found in Chapter 3.

General Catalogs

1. Books in Print (Title, Author, and Subject Indexes)
   - cost $92.50. for juveniles and adults. approx 300,000 materials (hardbounds, paperbacks, trade books, textbooks). published 1978; revised annually. title, author, and subject indexes published as separate volumes.
   - R. R. Bowker, P.O. Box 1807, Ann Arbor, MI 48106.

2. Catalog of NIE Education Products (Two Volumes)
   - cost $10.00 (vol. 1); $12.00 (vol. 2). all grade levels. 660 products funded, in whole or in part, by the National Institute of Education. published 1975.
   - U.S. Government Printing Office, Washington, D.C. 20402.

3. Educational Programs That Work
   - cost $4.95. all grade levels. approx 200 materials. fourth edition published 1977.
   - Order Department, Far West Laboratory for Educational Research and Development, 1855 Folsom St., San Francisco, CA 94103.

4. Educators Index of Free Materials
   - cost $33.00. high school level. approx 3000 materials. 87th edition published 1978; revised annually.
   - Educators Progress Service, Randolph, WI 53956.

5. El-Hi Textbooks in Print (Subject, Title, and Author Indexes)
   - cost $29.95. all grade levels. approx 15,000 materials. 106th edition published 1978; revised annually.
   - R. R. Bowker, P.O. Box 1807, Ann Arbor, MI 48106.

6. The First Catalog for Humanizing Education: 1978–9 Edition.
   - cost $5.95. all grade levels. approx 700 materials. published 1979.
   - National Humanistic Education Center, 110 Spring Street, Saratoga Springs, N.Y. 12866.

7. A Guide to Non-Sexist Children's Books
   - cost $7.95. all grade levels. approx 500 materials. published 1976.
   - Academy Press Ltd., 360 N. Michigan Ave., Chicago, IL 60601.

8. The Guide to Simulations/Games for Education and Training
- cost $49.95.   all grade levels.   approx 1100 materials.   fourth edition published 1980.   (library edition combines volume 1, academic games; and volume 2, business games).
- Sage Publications, P.O. Box 5024, Beverly Hills, CA 90210

9. Programmed Learning and Individually Paced Instruction Bibliography
- cost $70.00.   all grade levels.   several thousand materials.   fifth edition published 1978.
- Hendershot Programmed Learning Consultants, 4114 Ridgewood Dr., Bay City, MI 48706.

10. Selected Free Materials for Classroom Teachers
- cost $2.75.   all grade levels.   approx 2000 materials.   sixth edition published 1978.
- Fearon-Pitman Publishers, 6 Davis Dr., Belmont, CA 94002.

General Catalogs: *Nonprint Media*

11. Index to 8mm Motion Cartridges
- cost $47.00 ($2.50 for microfiche).   all grade levels.   approx 26,000 materials.   fifth edition published 1977.
- National Information Center for Educational Media, University of Southern California, University Park, Los Angeles, CA 90007.

12. Index to 16mm Educational Films
- cost $109.50 ($67.50 for microfiche).   all grade levels.   approx 100,-000 materials.   sixth edition published 1977.
- National Information Center for Educational Media, University of Southern California, University Park, Los Angeles, CA 90007.

13. Index to 35mm Filmstrips
- cost $86.50 ($45.50 for microfiche).   all grade levels.   approx 70,000 materials.   sixth edition published 1977.
- National Information Center for Educational Media, University of Southern California, University Park, Los Angeles, CA 90007.

14. Index to Educational Audio Tapes
- cost $47.00 ($23.50 for microfiche).   all grade levels.   approx 28,000 materials.   fourth edition published 1977.
- National Information Center for Educational Media, University of Southern California, University Park, Los Angeles, CA 90007.

15. Index to Educational Overhead Transparencies
- cost $75.50 ($39.50 for microfiche).   all grade levels.   approx 50,000 materials.   fifth edition published 1977.
- National Information Center for Educational Media, University of Southern California, University Park, Los Angeles, CA 90007.

16. Index to Educational Records
    • cost $47.00 ($23.50 for microfiche).   all grade levels.   approx 25,000 materials.   fourth edition published 1977.
    • National Information Center for Educational Media, University of Southern California, University Park, Los Angeles, CA 90007.

17. Index to Educational Slides
    • cost $42.50 ($22.00 for microfiche).   all grade levels.   approx 28,000 materials.   third edition published 1977.
    • National Information Center for Educational Media, University of Southern California, University Park, Los Angeles, CA 90007.

18. Index to Educational Video Tapes
    • cost $29.50 ($14.50 for microfiche).   all grade levels.   approx 15,000 materials.   fourth edition published 1977.
    • National Information Center for Educational Media, University of Southern California, University Park, Los Angeles, CA 90007.

19. Positive Images: A Guide to 400 Non-Sexist Films for Young People
    • cost $5.50.   all grade levels.   approx 400 materials.   published 1976.
    • Booklegger Press, 555 29th Street, San Francisco, CA 94131.

General Catalogs: Specific Age or Grade Levels

20. Children's Books in Print (Author, Title, and Illustrator Indexes)
    • cost $29.95.   elementary school levels.   approx 39,000 materials. published 1979; revised annually.
    • R. R. Bowker, P.O. Box 1807, Ann Arbor, MI 48106.

21. Core Media Collection for Secondary Schools
    • cost $17.50.   high school level.   approx 2000 materials.   published 1975.
    • R. R. Bowker, P.O. Box 1807, Ann Arbor, MI 48106.

22. Early Childhood Curriculum Materials: An Annotated Bibliography
    • cost $7.95.   preschool and primary school levels.   approx 70 materials and programs.   published 1976.
    • Special Learning Corporation, 42 Boston Post Road, Guilford, CT. 06437.

23. Early Learning Kits: 25 Evaluations (EPIE Report No. 68)
    • cost $20.00.   preschool and primary grade levels.   25 materials. published 1975.
    • EPIE Institute, 475 Riverside Drive, NYC, NY 10027.

24. Educators Grade Guide to Free Teaching Aids
    • cost $27.50.   elementary and junior high school levels.   approx 2000 materials.   24th edition published 1978; revised annually.
    • Educators Progress Service, Randolph, WI 53956.

25. The Elementary School Library Collection
   • cost $32.95.   primary and elementary school levels.   approx 2000 materials.   11th edition published 1977.
   • Bro-Dart, Newark, N.J.

26. Free and Inexpensive Materials for Preschool and Early Childhood
   • cost $4.50.   primary school level.   approx 600 materials.   second edition published 1977.
   • Fearon-Pitman Publishers, 6 Davis Dr., Belmont, CA 94002.

27. Index to College Television Courseware: A Comprehensive Directory of Credit Courses and Concept Modules Distributed on Video Tape and Film
   • cost $15.00.   high school level.   approx 300 materials.   third edition published 1976.
   • Computerized Courseware Clearinghouse, University of Wisconsin, Green Bay, WI 54302.

28. Inservice Teacher Training Materials (EPIE Report No. 80)
   • cost $10.00.   adult level.   49 materials.   published 1977.
   • EPIE Institute, 475 Riverside Drive, NYC, NY 10027.

29. Junior High School Library Catalog
   • cost $42.00.   junior high school level.   approx 4000 materials.   third edition published 1975 (plus annual supplements).
   • H. W. Wilson, 950 University Ave., Bronx, N.Y. 10452.

30. More Films Kids Like: A Catalog of Short Films for Children
   • cost $8.95.   primary and intermediate school level.   approx 200 materials.   published 1977.
   • American Library Association, Chicago, IL 60611.

31. Senior High School Library Catalog
   • cost $50.00.   high school level.   approx 5000 materials.   eleventh edition published 1977.
   • H. W. Wilson, 950 University Ave., Bronx, N.Y. 10452.

The Arts

32. Films for Arts and Crafts
   • free.   all grade levels.   approx 600 materials.   published 1977.
   • Pennsylvania State University, Audio-Visual Services, University Park, PA 16802.

33. Films for Filmstudy
   • no cost.   high school level.   approx 500 materials.   third edition published 1976.

- Pennsylvania State University Audio-Visual Services, Willard Biulding, University Park, PA 16802.

Bilingual and Multicultural Education

34. Building Ethnic Collections: An Annotated Guide for School Media Centers and Public Libraries
    - cost $18.50.   all grade levels.   approx 2300 materials.   published 1977.
    - Libraries Unlimited, P.O. Box 263, Littleton, CO 80160.

35. Ethnic American Minorities: A Guide to Media and Materials
    - cost $16.50.   all grade levels.   approx 1100 materials.   published 1976.
    - R. R. Bowker, P.O. Box 1807, Ann Arbor, MI 48106.

36. Latino Materials: A Multimedia Guide for Children and Young Adults
    - cost $14.95.   all grade levels.   approx 500 materials.   published 1979.
    - American Bibliographical Center — Clio Press, Riviera Press, 2040 A.P.S., Box 4397, Santa Barbara, CA 93103.

37. Materials and Human Resources for Teaching Ethnic Studies: An Annotated Bibliography
    - cost $7.95.   all grade levels.   approx 300 materials.   published 1975.
    - Social Science Education Consortium, 855 Broadway, Boulder, CO 80302.

38. A Selected and Annotated Bibliography of Bicultural Classroom Materials for Mexican American Studies
    - cost $6.00.   all grade levels.   278 materials.   published 1977.
    - R & E Research Associates, 4843 Mission St., San Francisco, CA 94112.

39. Selector's Guide for Bilingual Education Programs: Spanish "Branch" Programs (EPIE Report No. 74)
    - cost $10.00.   all grade levels.   76 materials + 11 materials for teachers.   published 1976.
    - EPIE Institute, 475 Riverside Drive, NYC, NY 10027.

40. Selector's Guide for Bilingual Education Materials: Spanish Language Arts (EPIE Report No. 73).
    - cost $10.00.   all grade levels.   70 materials + 8 materials for teachers.   published 1976.
    - EPIE Institute, 475 Riverside Drive, NYC, NY 10027.

Career and Consumer Education

41. Career Index
    - cost $10.00.   high school level.   approx 1500 materials for career education.   published 1978; revised annually.
    - Chronicle Guidance Publications, Inc., Moravia, NY 13118.

42. EPIE Career Education Selection and Evaluation Tools: Volume 2. Analyses of Seven Hundred Prescreened Materials.
    - cost $31.00 (both volumes).   all grade levels.   700 materials.   published 1975. (See also: Volume 1. How to Select and Evaluate Instructional Materials.)
    - EPIE Institute, 475 Riverside Drive, NYC, NY 10027.

43. A Guide to Free and Inexpensive Consumer Education Resources
    - cost available from ERIC.   high school level.   several thousand materials.   published 1976.
    - ERIC: ED 130 949.

44. A Resource Directory of Selected Consumer Education Materials for Grades K–8
    - free.   grades K–8.   approx 75 materials.   published 1976.
    - Illinois Office of Education, Program Planning and Development Section, Springfield, IL 62777.   (or from ERIC: ED 135 721)

English, Language Arts, and Reading

45. Reading and Language Arts: Products from NIE
    - cost $2.20.   all grade levels.   approx 75 materials.   published 1977.
    - Superintendent of Documents, U.S. Government Printing Office, Washington, D.C. 20401   (order number: S/N 017-080-01759-8)

46. Selected Print and Nonprint Resources in Speech Communication: An Annotated Bibliography K–12.
    - cost $2.50.   all grade levels.   approx 150 materials.   published 1976.
    - Speech Communication Association, 5205 Leesburg Pike, Falls Church, VA 22041.   (or from ERIC: ED 120 892)

47. Selected Sound Recordings of American, British and European Literature in English.
    - cost $10.00.   high school level.   approx 1400 materials.   published 1976.
    - Technological Media Center, University of Toledo, 2801 W. Bancroft Street, Toledo, OH 43606.   (or from ERIC: ED 130 631)

48. Selector's Guide for Elementary School Language Arts Programs (EPIE Report No. 78)

• cost $20.00. elementary school level. 11 materials. published 1977.

• EPIE Institute, 475 Riverside Drive, NYC, NY 10027.

49. Selector's Guide for Elementary School Reading Programs (EPIE Reports Nos. 82m and 83m)

• cost $40.00 ($20.00 per report). elementary school level. 24 materials. published 1977–1978.

• EPIE Institute, 475 Riverside Drive, NYC, NY 10027.

Foreign Languages

50. Bibliography of Audiovisual Instructional Materials for the Teaching of Spanish.

• cost $0.75. all grade levels. approx 400 materials. published 1975.

• California State Department of Education, 721 Capitol Mall, Sacramento, CA 95814. (or from ERIC: ED 119 508)

51. Bibliography of Instructional Materials for the Teaching of German.

• cost $0.75. all grade levels. approx 200 materials. published 1975.

• California State Department of Education, 721 Capitol Mall, Sacramento, CA 95814. (or from ERIC: ED 112 611)

52. Master Locator Booklet for Classroom Materials in TESOL.

• cost $4.05. all grade levels. approx 300 materials. third edition published 1975.

• Indiana University Linguistics Club, 310 Lindley Hall, Indiana University, Bloomington, IN 47401. (or from ERIC: ED 123 929)

Mathematics and Science

53. AAAS Science Book List Supplement.

• cost $16.50. all grade levels. approx 8000 materials. published 1978. (supplement for: *AAAS Science Book List for Children*, third edition, published 1972).

• American Association for the Advancement of Science, 1515 Massachusetts Ave., N.W., Washington, D.C. 20005.

54. AAAS Science Film Catalog.

• cost $18.50. all grade levels. approx 5600 materials. published 1975; updated in *Science Books and Films* published by AAAS four times annually (cost $16.00/year).

• R. R. Bowker, P.O. Box 1807, Ann Arbor, MI 48106.

55. Analyses of Elementary School Mathematics Materials (EPIE Report No. 69/70).

• cost $20.00. elementary school level. 32 materials. published 1975.

• EPIE Institute, 475 Riverside Drive, NYC, NY 10027.

56. Educators Guide to Free Science Materials

• cost $12.75. all grade levels. approx 1800 materials. 19th edition published 1978; revised annually.

• Educators Progress Service, Randolph, WI 53956.

57. Selector's Guide for Elementary School/Junior High School Science Programs (EPIE Report No. 77).

• cost $20.00. elementary and junior high school levels. 15 materials. published 1976.

• EPIE Institute, 475 Riverside Drive, NYC, NY 10027.

58. Selector's Guide for Secondary School Science Programs (EPIE Report No. 81).

• cost $20.00. high school level. 16 materials. published 1977.

• EPIE Institute, 475 Riverside Drive, NYC, NY 10027.

Mental Health, Physical Health, Recreation, Religion, and Safety

59. About Aging: A Catalog of Films.

• cost $3.50. intermediate and high school levels. approx 400 materials. third edition published 1977.

• Andrus Gerontology Center, University of Southern California, Los Angeles, CA 90007.

60. Bible-Related Curriculum Materials: A Bibliography

• cost $5.95. high school level. approx 300 materials. published 1976.

• Abingdon Press, 201 Eighth Avenue South, Nashville, TN 37202.

61. A Bibliography of Drug Abuse: Including Alcohol and Tobacco.

• cost $15.00. all grade levels. approx 700 materials. published 1977.

• Libraries Unlimited, P.O. Box 263, Littleton, CO 80160.

62. The Bookfinder: A Guide to Children's Literature About the Needs and Problems of Youth Aged 2–15.

• cost $28.50. preschool through junior high school. approx 1000 materials. published 1977.

• American Guidance Service, Publishers' Building, Circle Pines, MN 55014.

63. A Comprehensive Resource Guide to 16mm Mental Health Films.

• cost $25.00. all grade levels. approx 1500 materials. published 1977.

• Mental Health Media Evaluation Project, P.O. Box 1548, Springfield, VA 22151.

64. Educators Guide to Free Guidance Materials.

• cost $13.00. high school level. approx 2000 materials. 17th edition published 1978; revised annually.

• Educators Progress Service, Randolph, WI 53956.

65. Educators Guide to Free Health, Physical Education and Recreation Materials.

• cost $13.50. all grade levels. approx 2500 materials. 11th edition published 1978; revised annually.

• Educators Progress Service, Randolph, WI 53956.

66. Film Resources for Sex Education.

• cost $4.95. all grade levels. approx 200 materials. published 1976.

• Sex Information Council of the U.S., Human Sciences Press, 72 Fifth Avenue, New York, NY 10001.

67. Guide to Free-Loan Sports Films (16 mm).

• cost $6.95. all grade levels. approx 500 materials. second edition published 1975.

• Serina Press, Alexandria, VA 22305.

68. Index to Health and Safety Education: Multimedia.

• cost $47.00 ($23.50 for microfiche). all grade levels. approx 33,000 materials. third edition published 1977.

• National Information Center for Educational Media, University of Southern California, University Park, Los Angeles, CA 90007.

Social Studies

69. Alternatives in Print: Catalog of Social Change Publications

• cost $12.95. high school level. approx 10,000 materials. fifth edition published 1977.

• New Glide Publications, 330 Ellis St., San Francisco, CA 94102.

70. Cities

• cost $19.95. all grade levels. approx 200 materials. published 1976.

• R. R. Bowker, P.O. Box 1807, Ann Arbor, MI 48106.

71. Educators Guide to Free Social Studies Materials

• cost $13.75. all grade levels. approx 3900 materials. 18th edition published 1978; revised annually.

• Educators Progress Service, Randolph, WI 53956.

72. Energy: A Multimedia Guide for Children and Young Adults
    - cost $14.95. all grade levels. several hundred materials. published 1979.
    - American Bibliographical Center — Clio Press, Riviera Campus, 2040 A.P.S., Box 4397, Santa Barbara, CA 93103.

73. Films for Anthropological Teaching.
    - cost $5.00. high school level. approx 800 materials. sixth edition published 1977.
    - American Anthropological Association, 1703 New Hampshire Ave., N.W., Washington, D.C. 20009.

74. Films on the Future: A Selective History.
    - cost $6.00. junior high and high school levels. approx 250 materials. published 1977.
    - World Future Society, 4916 St. Elmo Avenue, Washington, D.C. 20014.

75. Index to Environmental Studies (Multi-Media)
    - cost $34.50 ($18.50 for microfiche). all grade levels. approx 26,000 materials. published 1977.
    - National Information Center for Educational Media, University of Southern California, University Park, Los Angeles, CA 90007.

76. Index to Psychology — Multimedia
    - cost $47.00 ($23.50 for microfiche). all grade levels. approx 28,000 materials. third edition published 1977.
    - National Information Center for Educational Media, University of Southern California, University Park, Los Angeles, CA 90007.

77. Media: An Annotated Catalogue of Law-Related Audio-Visual Materials.
    - free. all grade levels. approx 400 materials. published 1975.
    - American Bar Association, 1155 East 60th Street, Chicago, IL 60637.

78. Secondary School Social Studies: Analyses of 31 Programs (EPIE Report No. 71).
    - cost $20.00. high school level. 31 materials. published 1976.
    - EPIE Institute, 475 Riverside Drive, NYC, NY 10027.

79. Selector's Guide for Elementary School Social Studies Programs (EPIE Report No. 84m).
    - cost $20.00. elementary school level. 10 materials. published 1978.
    - EPIE Institute, 475 Riverside Drive, NYC, NY 10027.

80. Selector's Guide for High School United States History Programs (EPIE Report No. 87m).
    - cost $20.00. high school level. 11 materials. published 1979.
    - EPIE Institute, 475 Riverside Drive, NYC, NY 10027.

81. Social Studies Curriculum Materials Data Book.

    - cost $75.00 (supplements $20.00 annually). all grade levels. approx 300 materials. data books are updated twice annually.
    - Social Science Education Consortium, 855 Broadway, Boulder, CO 80302.

82. Teacher's Resource Handbook for African Studies: An Annotated Bibliography of Curriculum Materials Preschool Through Grade Twelve.

    - cost $1.50. all grade levels. approx 650 materials. published 1976.
    - African Studies Center, University of California, Los Angeles, CA 90024. (or from ERIC: ED 137 213).

83. Teacher's Resource Handbook for Asian Studies: An Annotated Bibliography of Curriculum Materials, Preschool Through Grade Twelve.

    - cost $3.00. all grade levels. approx 700 materials. published 1976.
    - Curriculum Inquiry Center, Graduate School of Education, University of California, 405 Hilgard Ave., Los Angeles, CA 90024. (or from ERIC: ED 133 241).

84. Teacher's Resource Handbook for Latin American Studies: Annotated Bibliography of Curriculum Materials, Preschool Through Grade Twelve.

    - cost $2.50. all grade levels. approx 1300 materials. published 1975.
    - Curriculum Inquiry Center, Graduate School of Education, University of California, 405 Hilgard Ave., Los Angeles, CA 90024. (or from ERIC: ED 133 239).

85. Teacher's Resource Handbook for Near-Eastern Studies: An Annotated Bibliography of Curriculum Materials, Preschool Through Grade Twelve.

    - cost $2.50. all grade levels. approx 800 materials. published 1976.
    - Curriculum Inquiry Center, Graduate School of Education, University of California, 405 Hilgard Ave., Los Angeles, CA 90024. (or from ERIC: ED 133 242).

86. Teacher's Resource Handbook for Russian and East European Studies: An Annotated Bibliography of Curriculum Materials Preschool Through Grade Twelve.

    - cost $2.50. all grade levels. approx 700 materials. published 1976.
    - Curriculum Inquiry Center, Graduate School of Education, University of California, 405 Hilgard Ave., Los Angeles, CA 90024. (or from ERIC: ED 133 240).

Special Education: Handicapped and Gifted

87. Handbook of Instructional Resources and References for Teaching the Gifted.

• cost $13.95. all grade levels. approx 650 materials. published 1980.

• Allyn and Bacon, Longwood Division, Rockleigh, NJ 07647

88. Master Catalog of NIMIS/NICSEM Special Education Information Volumes I and II.

• cost $121.00. all grade levels. approx 36,000 materials. published 1979. (four other volumes contain subsets of materials listed in the Master Catalog: Index to Media and Materials for the Deaf, Hard of Hearing, Speech Impaired, cost $60.00; Index to Media and Materials for the Mentally Retarded, Specific Learning Disabled, Emotionally Disturbed, cost $55.00; Index to Media and Materials for the Visually Handicapped, Orthopedically Impaired, Other Health Impaired, cost $40.00; Index to Assessment Devices, Testing Instruments and Parent Materials, cost $33.00).

• University of Southern California, NICSEM, University Park (RAN) 2nd Floor, Los Angeles, CA 90007.

89. Special Education Index to Learner Materials.

• cost $60.00. all grade levels. approx 10,000 materials. published 1979.

• The National Information Center for Educational Media, University of Southern California, University Park, Los Angeles, CA 90007.

90. Teacher Training in Mainstreaming (EPIE Report No. 86m).

• cost $20.00. adult level. 15 materials. published 1978.

• EPIE Institute, 475 Riverside Drive, NYC, NY 10027.

Vocational and Technical Education

91. A Bibliography of Free Loan Materials for Agriculture Education.

• cost available from ERIC. high school level. approx 900 materials. third edition published 1976; revised annually.

• Wisconsin Vocational Studies Center, University of Wisconsin, Madison, WI 53706. (or from ERIC: ED 132 279).

92. A Bibliography of Free Loan Materials for Business Education.

• cost available from ERIC. high school level. approx 500 materials. third edition published 1976; revised annually.

• Wisconsin Vocational Studies Center, University of Wisconsin, Madison, WI 53706. (or from ERIC: ED 132 274).

93. A Bibliography of Free Loan Materials for Distributive Education.

• cost available from ERIC.   high school level.   approx 500 materials. third edition published 1976; revised annually.

• Wisconsin Vocational Studies Center, University of Wisconsin, Madison, WI 53706.   (or from ERIC: ED 132 277).

94. A Bibliography of Free Loan Materials for Health Occupations Education.

   • cost available from ERIC.   high school level.   approx 500 materials. third edition published 1976; revised annually.

   • Wisconsin Vocational Studies Center, University of Wisconsin, Madison, WI 53706.   (or from ERIC: ED 132 275).

95. A Bibliography of Free Loan Materials for Trade and Industrial Education.

   • cost available from ERIC.   high school level.   approx 1000 materials.   third edition published 1976; revised annually.

   • Wisconsin Vocational Studies Center, University of Wisconsin, Madison, WI 53706.   (or from ERIC: ED 132 276).

96. Index to Vocational and Technical Education (Multimedia)

   • cost $47.00 ($23.50 for microfiche).   all grade levels.   approx 32,000 materials.   third edition published 1977.

   • National Information Center for Educational Media, University of Southern California, University Park, Los Angeles, CA 90007.

Appendix D
Inventory of Evaluation Criteria
Stated as Questions

Publication and Cost

1. Authors: *Are the authors known and respected professionally?*

2. Cost: *Is the cost of the materials reasonable relative to other, comparable materials?*

3. Development History: *Were the materials adequately field tested and revised prior to publication?*

4. Edition: *Is this edition to be in publication for several years, or is a new edition to be released shortly?*

5. Publication Date: *Were these materials published within the last two years?*

6. Publisher: *Does the publisher of these materials have a good reputation among educators?*

7. Purchase Procedures: *Are the purchase procedures clear and easy to use?*

8. Quantity: *Are there likely to be difficulties in obtaining sufficient quantities of the materials for each student who will be using them?*

9. Special Requirements: *Do our schools have the special resources required for use of the materials?*

10. Teacher Training: *Does use of the materials require skills that our district teachers are not likely to possess?*

Physical Properties

11. Aesthetic Appeal: *Are the materials likely to appeal to the user's aesthetic sense?*

12. Components: *Do the materials contain so many components that teachers will have difficulty in keeping track of them and using them?*

13. Consumables: *Does the product make unnecessary use of consumable materials?*

14. Durability: *Do the materials have components that are especially vulnerable to wear?*

15. Media: *Does the developer make appropriate use of the media included among the materials?*

16. Quality: *Did the publisher use high quality materials in the production process?*

17. Safety: *Are there possible hazards to students or teachers in using the materials?*

Content

18. Approach: *Does the developer use an approach consistent with the district's curriculum?*

19. Instructional Objectives: *Are the materials' objectives compatible with the district's curriculum and acceptable to teachers?*

20. Instructional Objectives — Types: *Do the materials contain affective objectives in addition to cognitive objectives?*

21. Issues Orientation: *Are the materials free of biases that are misleading or that are likely to be unacceptable to teachers, students, and the community?*

22. Multiculturalism: *Do the materials reflect the contributions and perspectives of various ethnic and cultural groups?*

23. Scope and Sequence: *Are the scope and sequence of the materials compatible with the district's curriculum?*

24. Sex Roles: *Is the content of the materials free of sex stereotypes?*

25. Time-Boundedness: *Does the content of the materials reflect current knowledge and culture?*

Instructional Properties

26. Assessment Devices: *Do the materials contain tests and other assessment devices that will be helpful to the teacher and his or her students?*

27. Comprehensibility: *Will the materials be clearly understood by the students who will be using them?*

28. Coordination with the Curriculum: *Are the materials compatible with other materials currently being used in the school?*

29. Individualization: *Does the design of the materials allow teachers to use them differently according to student needs?*

30. Instructional Effectiveness: *Does the publisher provide any data on the effectiveness of the materials in actual use?*

31. Instructional Patterns: *Is the primary instructional pattern likely to help the learner achieve the materials' objectives?*

32. Learner Characteristics: *Are the materials appropriate for the students who will be using them?*

33. Length: *Are the materials an appropriate length so that they can fit conveniently into the teacher's instructional schedule?*

34. Management System: *Is the use of the materials easily managed by the teacher?*

35. Motivational Properties: *Are the materials likely to excite the interest of students and teachers?*

36. Prerequisites: *Are the students likely to have the prerequisite knowledge or skills necessary for learning the content of the materials?*

37. Readability: *Are the materials written at an appropriate reading level for students who will be using them?*

38. Role of the Student: *Do the materials include activities that students are capable of doing and that they will enjoy doing?*

39. Role of the Teacher: *Do the materials include activities that teachers will find interesting and rewarding?*

Appendix E
Features of Curriculum Materials
That May Facilitate Learning

1. **Advance Organizer.** A preview, usually in the form of an introductory paragraph, that gives the learner a conceptual framework for assimilating the learning experience to follow.

2. **Clarity.** The clear presentation, to the learner, of vocabulary, syntax, concepts, examples, and content organization.

3. **Cueing.** Items pointing to information and ideas important for the learner to understand and remember. Cueing can be in the form of headings, margin notes, use of contrasting typeface, or explicit statements telling the learner that a particular fact or idea is important.

4. **Diagnostic Tests.** An assessment procedure for indicating skill areas in which the student has strengths or weaknesses. Diagnostic tests provide the basis for individualized instruction.

5. **Enthusiasm.** A communication style that conveys the excitement of a particular field of knowledge to the learner. Tone of voice (e.g., in an instructional film) and personalized writing style are techniques for projecting enthusiasm.

6. **Examples.** Particular facts, instances, or aspects to illustrate a more general concept or principle.

7. **Feedback.** Procedures for providing information to learners on the quality or accuracy of their performance in practicing new knowledge and skills.

8. **Glossary.** A list of unfamiliar and technical terms presented in the curriculum materials so that the learner can focus attention on them.

9. **Independence Level.** Inclusion of instructional experiences appropriate for the learner's level of independence.

10. **Inserted Questions.** Placement of questions before, in, or after an instructional message to help the learner engage in "active" reading, viewing, or listening.

11. **Manipulatives and Realia.** Objects or activities used to relate classroom teaching to real life.

12. **Models** Descriptions or analogies used to help the learner visualize something that cannot be directly observed.

13. **Objectives.** Explicit statement of an instructional unit's goals so that the learner knows beforehand what knowledge and skills he or she needs to master.

14. **Outline.** A summary of the main ideas and their sequence in an instructional unit; the purpose of which is to cue the learner to these ideas and to provide a framework for organizing them.

15. **Perceived Purpose.** Presentation to the learner of reasons for studying a particular unit of instructional content.

16. **Practice.** Opportunity for the learner to rehearse the knowledge or skills contained in an instructional unit.

17. **Prerequisites.** Explicit statement of the knowledge and skills needed by the learner if he or she is to profit from a particular instructional experience.

18. **Recycling.** Opportunity for the learner to restudy an instructional unit if he or she fails a corresponding test.

19. **Reinforcers.** Provision of an extrinsic reward (e.g., tokens, praise, grades, a pleasurable activity) to the learner upon successful completion of an instructional experience.

20. **Self-Check Test.** An assessment device that enables the learner to check his or her level of mastery. Results of the self-check test are not used as a formal evaluation of the learner's performance by the teacher.

21. **Variety.** Several different instructional strategies, formats, and media used to convey instructional content.

Index

About the Author

Professor Meredith D. Gall received his Ph.D. from the University of California at Berkeley. He is a professor in the Department of Curriculum and Instruction at the University of Oregon, Eugene, and is Director of Graduate Programs in Teacher Education. Professor Gall is author and co-author of many books, articles, and papers in education.